Wilfrid Laurier

Wilfrid Laurier

by ANDRÉ PRATTE

With an Introduction by
John Ralston Saul
SERIES EDITOR

English translation by
Phyllis Aronoff and Howard Scott

EXTRAORDINARY
CANADIANS

PENGUIN CANADA

Published by the Penguin Group

Penguin Group (Canada), 90 Eglinton Avenue East, Suite 700,
Toronto, Ontario, Canada M4P 2Y3 (a division of Pearson Canada Inc.)

Penguin Group (USA) Inc., 375 Hudson Street, New York, New York 10014, U.S.A.
Penguin Books Ltd, 80 Strand, London WC2R 0RL, England
Penguin Ireland, 25 St Stephen's Green, Dublin 2, Ireland (a division of Penguin Books Ltd)
Penguin Group (Australia), 250 Camberwell Road, Camberwell, Victoria 3124, Australia
(a division of Pearson Australia Group Pty Ltd)
Penguin Books India Pvt Ltd, 11 Community Centre, Panchsheel Park,
New Delhi – 110 017, India
Penguin Group (NZ), 67 Apollo Drive, Rosedale, North Shore 0745, Auckland, New Zealand
(a division of Pearson New Zealand Ltd)
Penguin Books (South Africa) (Pty) Ltd, 24 Sturdee Avenue, Rosebank,
Johannesburg 2196, South Africa
Penguin Books Ltd, Registered Offices: 80 Strand, London WC2R 0RL, England

First published 2011

1 2 3 4 5 6 7 8 9 10 (RRD)

Manufactured in the U.S.A.

LIBRARY AND ARCHIVES CANADA CATALOGUING IN PUBLICATION

Pratte, André, 1957-
Wilfrid Laurier / André Pratte.

(Extraordinary Canadians)
ISBN 978-0-670-06918-7

1. Laurier, Wilfrid, Sir, 1841-1919. 2. Canada—Politics and
government—1896-1911. 3. Prime ministers—Canada—Biography.
I. Title. II. Series: Extraordinary Canadians

FC551.L3P73 2011   971.05'6092   C2010-907115-8

Visit the Penguin Group (Canada) website at **www.penguin.ca**

Special and corporate bulk purchase rates available; please see
www.penguin.ca/corporatesales or call 1-800-810-3104, ext. 2477 or 2474

This book was printed on 30% PCW recycled paper

CONTENTS

John Ralston Saul

How do civilizations imagine themselves? One way is for each of us to look at ourselves through our society's most remarkable figures. I'm not talking about hero worship or political iconography. That is a danger to be avoided at all costs. And yet people in every country do keep on going back to the most important people in their past.

This series of Extraordinary Canadians brings together rebels, reformers, martyrs, writers, painters, thinkers, political leaders. Why? What is it that makes them relevant to us so long after their deaths?

For one thing, their contributions are there before us, like the building blocks of our society. More important than that are their convictions and drive, their sense of what is right and wrong, their willingness to risk all, whether it be their lives, their reputations, or simply being wrong in public. Their ideas, their triumphs and failures, all of these somehow constitute a mirror of our society. We look at these people, all dead, and discover what we have been, but also what we can be. A mirror is an instrument for measuring ourselves. What we see can be both a warning and an encouragement.

These eighteen biographies of twenty key Canadians are centred on the meaning of each of their lives. Each of them is very different, but these are not randomly chosen great figures. Together they produce a grand sweep of the creation of modern Canada, from our first steps as a democracy in 1848 to our questioning of modernity late in the twentieth century.

All of them except one were highly visible on the cutting edge of their day while still in their twenties, thirties, and forties. They were young, driven, curious. An astonishing level of fresh energy surrounded them and still does. We in the twenty-first century talk endlessly of youth, but power today is often controlled by people who fear the sort of risks and innovations embraced by everyone in this series. A number of them were dead—hanged, infected on a battlefield, broken by their exertions—well before middle age. Others hung on into old age, often profoundly dissatisfied with themselves.

Each one of these people has changed you. In some cases you know this already. In others you will discover how through these portraits. They changed the way the world hears music, thinks of war, communicates. They changed how each of us sees what surrounds us, how minorities are treated, how we think of immigrants, how we look after each other, how we imagine ourselves through what are now our stories.

You will notice that many of them were people of the word. Not just the writers. Why? Because civilizations are built around many themes, but they require a shared public language. So Laurier, Bethune, Douglas, Riel, LaFontaine, McClung, Trudeau, Lévesque, Big Bear, even Carr and Gould, were masters of the power of language. Beaverbrook was one of the most powerful newspaper publishers of his day. Countries need action and laws and courage. But civilization is not a collection of prime ministers. Words, words, words—it is around these that civilizations create and imagine themselves.

The authors I have chosen for each subject are not the obvious experts. They are imaginative, questioning minds from among our leading writers and activists. They have, each one of them, a powerful connection to their subject. And in their own lives, each is engaged in building what Canada is now becoming.

That is why a documentary is being filmed around each subject. Images are yet another way to get at each subject and to understand their effect on us.

The one continuous, essential voice of biography since 1961 has been the *Dictionary of Canadian Biography*. But there has not been a project of book-length biographies such as Extraordinary Canadians in a hundred years, not since the Makers of Canada series. And yet every generation understands the past differently, and so sees in the mirror of these remarkable figures somewhat different lessons. As history rolls on, some truths remain the same while others are revealed in a new and unexpected way.

What strikes me again and again is just how dramatically ethical decisions figured in these people's lives. They form the backbone of history and memory. Some of them, Big Bear, for example, or Dumont, or even Lucy Maud Montgomery, thought of themselves as failures by the end of their lives. But the ethical cord that was strung taut through their work has now carried them on to a new meaning and even greater strength, long after their deaths.

Each of these stories is a revelation of the tough choices unusual people must make to find their way. And each of us as readers will find in the desperation of the Chinese revolution, the search for truth in fiction, the political and military dramas, different meanings that strike a personal chord. At first it is that personal emotive link to such figures which draws us in. Then we find they are a key that opens the whole society of their time to us. Then we realize that in that 150-year period many of them knew each other, were friends, opposed each other. Finally, when all these stories are put together, you will see that a whole new debate has been created around Canadian civilization and the shape of our continuous experiment.

So much of this experiment has depended on *the word* and the creation of new political ideas. Wilfrid Laurier was a man of the word. His speeches and his way of talking to people were all built upon the non-violent philosophy of LaFontaine and Baldwin and were central to his political success. He created a new chapter of compromise, which would stumble several times, particularly during the First World War, but would recover to shape the Canada of the twentieth century. André Pratte understands the battles Laurier fought, using the weapons of intelligence, oratory, and his "Sunny Ways." Pratte, himself an important voice for social compromise, brings a sharp and modern clarity to a leader who set the stage for modern Canada.

Wilfrid Laurier

Forgotten

> Perhaps history may be the pillar of cloud by day and the
>   pillar of fire by night
> To show us the way and give us the light.
> **WILFRID LAURIER, 1905**

Quebec City, at the corner of Charest and Langelier boule-
vards, in the heart of what they call the Lower Town, at the
boundary between two old working-class neighbourhoods in
the province's capital. Here, on a raised platform across from
a service station, we find a statue of Wilfrid Laurier, leader
of the Liberal Party of Canada from 1887 to 1919 and prime
minister of Canada from 1896 to 1911.

Why did they choose such a sad, banal site for a
monument to one of the most important politicians in
Canadian history? It is so isolated that the tourist walking
route through the neighbourhood does not even mention it.
According to the city's cultural department, the statue was
erected in 1954. It is a copy of one commissioned by the
Laurier Memorial Committee the year before for Dorchester
Square in Montreal, and was created by the famous sculptor

Émile Brunet, who a quarter century earlier had been given the task of immortalizing the former prime minister on Parliament Hill in Ottawa.

Dorchester Square was the obvious choice: it was in the downtown core of the province of Quebec's metropolis and it was already home to many statues, including one of the first prime minister of the new confederation, John A. Macdonald. But in Quebec City, why choose Langelier Boulevard? I had to do some digging in order to understand: this spot is in what was formerly the riding of Quebec East, which Wilfrid Laurier represented in the House of Commons for forty-two years. Among the many dignitaries present at the unveiling of the statue was one of his successors as member of Parliament for Quebec East and prime minister of Canada, Louis St-Laurent.

Strangely enough, the monument's sponsors did not consider it necessary to put up a plaque explaining the choice of the site and reminding passersby who Wilfrid Laurier was. The only word inscribed on the pedestal of the statue is LAURIER. To Laurier's admirers, it was probably sufficient to erect a monument to the great man and recall his name. LAURIER—why say anything more? Didn't all Canadians know who Laurier was?

In the 1950s, that might have been true, but certainly not

today. On the contrary, it is likely that the vast majority of people stopping at this statue have only a vague idea of the crucial role the man it represents played in our history. In November 2008, the Dominion Institute, an organization devoted to making the history of our country better known, asked a sample of Canadians this simple question: "What French Canadian prime minister famously proclaimed, 'The twentieth century will belong to Canada'?" The results were terribly disappointing. Only 25 percent of Canadians could give the correct answer. Barely 22 percent of Quebecers recognized the words of one of the most illustrious figures in their history.

These results are deplorable, since they show how ignorant Canadians are of their country's past. And they do not augur well for the future of Canada. Knowledge of history is crucial when a people has to overcome the difficulties of the present and choose a path for the future. By studying history, we can reconnect with the ideals and values that inspired our forebears. We can observe without complacency that what divides us is old and painful, but above all, we can realize that what unites us has always triumphed. Those victories were improbable and they were hard won. The future is not guaranteed. However, there are many lessons we can learn from Laurier, lessons that are as valuable today as they were a century ago. These teachings emerge from what he was and what he did.

Even more than his predecessors, Laurier had to confront the demons of intolerance and prejudice that constantly threatened the work of the Fathers of Confederation and that still rear their heads today. And it was Laurier who, better than anyone before or since, showed Canadians the only path possible, that of compromise. Today, as at that time, it is also the most arduous path, and those who follow it have more enemies than admirers, especially in the linguistic, religious, ethnic, or regional community they belong to, because they refuse to be confined by allegiance or to give in to emotion or narrow-mindedness. If Canada still exists today, it is because there have always been Canadians who felt that Laurier was right, that compromise is not surrender or cowardice, but rather daring and courage.

The Canada of Laurier's time was a country that was both simpler and more difficult than the Canada of today. Political debate was dominated by powerful ideologies that all had their extremists: ultramontanists, Orangemen, Grits, Rouges, and French Canadian nationalists. Choosing the path of reason or the middle course was both humanly demanding and politically risky. Laurier was able to do it for the fifteen years he held power by relying on three complementary strategies. First, he encouraged the nascent Canadian patriotism. He hoped, like George-Étienne Cartier, one of the Fathers of Confederation, that over the years a Canadian "political nationhood" would emerge that would unite the country's linguistic, religious, and regional groups around a common project, without erasing their distinctive features. Second, Laurier always put his faith in what he called the "sunny ways": dialogue, patience, respect, a sense of compromise. And finally, Laurier asked Canadians to go beyond their linguistic and cultural differences and be guided by higher principles: justice, democracy, and authentic federalism. A century later, these three strategies are still the only ones that will enable Canadians to continue their journey together in prosperity and peace.

Laurier's heritage is all the more valuable to us because the major issues he had to deal with are still at the heart of political debate on the present and future of Canada: relations between the anglophone majority and the francophone minority (which in Laurier's time were considered to be different "races," the British and the French); conflicts between civil society and religion; Canada's participation in armed conflicts in foreign lands; and relations, especially trade, with our powerful neighbour to the south. On each of these questions, Laurier made an original contribution, a blend of daring and wisdom that became a typically Canadian trait.

Laurier was a history buff. Whenever he was confronted with a new problem, he would immediately familiarize himself with its distant and recent background. That gave him a better understanding of both the real issues and the motives of those involved. His extensive knowledge of the past partly explains his legendary moderation. If Canadians today were better informed about their history, they would understand each other better and more easily find solutions to their common problems. We have in fact done rather well. But we could do even better. We need to do better, living in a society that is increasingly complex and diverse, and with old and new economic, social, and cultural problems that threaten to undermine our unity and our development.

If we knew our history, we would know that this extraordinary Canadian personified an ambitious vision of this country better than anyone since. And we would see him as a powerful inspiration for pursuing the extraordinary ideal called Canada.

CHAPTER 1

The Man

> I see the goal and towards that goal I direct my efforts,
> discarding the impetuous frowns of the rash, the cautious
> advice of the timid. How gladly I would give my place to
> someone else, if someone else would take it. Unfortunately
> I feel the coils tighter every day around me; true the coils
> are weaved in affection; they are none the less the coils of
> a very heavy chain.
> **WILFRID LAURIER TO ÉMILIE LAVERGNE, 1891**

Legend has left us a portrait of Sir Wilfrid Laurier that is magnificent but simplistic. He was "the first Canadian," the one who guided the young country's first steps toward independence. He was the great conciliator. The silver-tongued orator. The one who predicted that "the twentieth century will belong to Canada," and who did so much to make that prediction a reality. All this is true. However, the more we delve into Laurier's life and the extraordinary legacy he left, the more complex and paradoxical his character seems.

We get a hint of that in the epigraph above, which is taken from a letter to Émilie Lavergne, whom many have described as his mistress: he is determined to continue his work, but frail and exhausted; he feels a prisoner of his fate, but is incapable of conceiving of anyone else carrying on. Throughout his political career, Laurier dreamed of returning to the tranquility of his Arthabaska home. However, he let politics dominate his life until his last breath at the venerable age of seventy-seven.

His contemporaries themselves had trouble understanding Laurier. The task is even more difficult almost a century after his death, for someone who never met him or heard him speak. There are only a few photographs of him and a little bit of film footage. Some people have mentioned a recording of his voice, but I never found it. We must therefore today seek "the real Laurier" by reading what was said by his biographers, only a few of whom knew him (which does not necessarily mean that they are more reliable), and by studying his speeches and correspondence. Paper and ink, flat and dry, hide as much as they reveal.

THE SHADOW OF DEATH

Wilfrid Laurier was haunted by illness throughout his life. Tuberculosis killed his mother, Marcelle, when he was six years old. The same disease took his little sister, Malvina, at the age of eleven, and possibly his father as well. Laurier himself suffered from violent fits of coughing every fall. He was convinced that tuberculosis was stalking him, ready to cut him down. Dr. Séraphin Gauthier, whose house he lived in while attending law school in Montreal, diagnosed chronic bronchitis instead. Laurent-Olivier David, who became his closest friend, described him as a young lawyer: "a melancholy, sickly appearance.... We felt friendship toward him mixed with respect and sympathy, because he seemed to us to have the shadow of death upon his pale, sad face."

We will never know exactly what Laurier suffered from, although today it is generally thought to have been tuberculosis. Whatever the nature of the illness, its violent symptoms would afflict him periodically throughout his life. He spoke of "racking pains ... feverish, half-delirious nights." Sometimes he would spit blood. After he became prime minister, he at times had to withdraw from public life for weeks at a time to regain his strength.

Was it only a physical ailment? Reading about the periods when he lay on his bed delirious and exhausted, hearing of his constant threats to resign to return to the peaceful life of a lawyer, one cannot help wondering if in addition to his physical fragility, Laurier may have had a depressive side. However, David says he was one of the most constantly happy men he has ever known.

At any rate, throughout his time as leader of the Liberal Party, he complained that he felt unequal to the situation and dreamed of giving it up. Was this a way to make himself wanted, to make his troops submit when times were tough? Perhaps. However, his discouragement appears to have been sincere. It was certainly not political tactics that led him to speak of resignation to his friend Émilie: "I wish I could throw up that burden and go back to my profession." And further: "Here I am chained to this detested place for many weeks to come. I am thinking, planning to find a way to rid myself from this burden on my shoulders and go back to my profession."

One would expect a man who finds the cross so heavy to bear to leave his duties at the first setback, the first disappointment. But Wilfrid Laurier went through one trial after another, and in the end remained Liberal leader for thirty-one years. He became prime minister in 1896, and won the elections of 1900, 1904, and 1908. He did not quit after the Liberal defeat of 1911, nor even after that of 1917, against Borden's Union Government, which called into question his entire life's work. On the contrary, he redoubled his efforts despite his advanced age. Only death, in 1919, would tear the leadership of the Liberal Party from his hands. How can someone so unhappy with the job carry it out so doggedly?

What kept him from laying the burden down? Ambition? The secret pleasure he found in that mad occupation?

AN ATYPICAL CHILDHOOD

Wilfrid Laurier was born on November 20, 1841, in the village of Saint-Lin, thirty kilometres north of Montreal, a French Canadian village like hundreds of others at the time. His father, Carolus, was a surveyor. A few months after Marcelle's death, he married Adeline Éthier, who had until then been the servant in the house. Wilfrid loved his step-mother as if she were his biological mother. He had a happy childhood.

Carolus had high hopes for his son's success. He took a keen interest in politics; he was a Patriote sympathizer and was opposed to the union of the two Canadas that Lord Durham recommended. Still, he wanted Wilfrid to learn English. At the age of ten, the child left his village for New Glasgow, ten kilometres to the west, which had been founded forty years earlier by Scots Presbyterians. He stayed there for two years with the Murray and the Kirk families (respectively Presbyterians and Irish Catholics), returning to Saint-Lin every weekend and during the summer holidays.

John Murray, the owner of the general store in New Glasgow, and Carolus Laurier had become friends when

Carolus had surveyed the area around the village. Wilfrid liked to help Mr. Murray serve customers in the store. At the New Glasgow school, he came into contact with English literature. If childhood experiences form adult attitudes, those two years were decisive for Laurier. Not only did he learn English—it is said that he spoke it with a Scottish accent throughout his life—but he learned that the "other," the English, the Protestant, was not the devil. He learned tolerance.

Wilfrid went to secondary school some thirty kilometres east of Saint-Lin at the Collège de L'Assomption, which was founded in 1832. As in all the classical colleges of the time, instruction was strictly controlled by the very conservative Quebec Church. The program was study and prayer, starting at 5:25 in the morning. A serious student, Laurier had excellent marks. But the time was long and his visits home were rare. Occasionally he would evade the watchful eyes of the priests to attend a trial or a political meeting, spectacles that were enjoyed in the rural Quebec of the era.

Then, showing an unusual openness toward English Canada, Laurier studied law at McGill University in Montreal. One can imagine how unfamiliar it must have felt to him: Saint-Lin was an agricultural settlement of twenty-five hundred souls, while Montreal was an industrial city of ninety thousand. Nevertheless, the young man seemed to adapt easily. At McGill, as at college, he was near the top of his class. No doubt this is why, at the end of his three years of studies, he was asked to give the valedictory speech, in French, at the graduation ceremony. In this first speech of his life, Laurier showed the combination of idealism and naïveté that would always be his: "Two races share today the soil of Canada. I can say it here, for the time is no longer, the French and the English races have not always been friends; but I hasten to say it, and I say it to our glory, that race hatreds are finished on our Canadian soil. There is no longer any family here but the human family. It matters not the language people speak, or the altars at which they kneel." This idyllic image of the situation in the country was hardly in keeping with the reality of the time. At any rate, very few people of his "race" would have expressed such sentiments. Laurier was already an atypical French Canadian.

Laurier's adversaries often criticized him for his admiration for British institutions, and denigrated the slight English accent that, it was said, tinged his French. According to one of his biographers, Laurier LaPierre, the accent came from his teacher Rodolphe Laflamme, in whose office he articled. This habit of copying the English even when speaking their own language was for a long time widespread among the French Canadian bourgeoisie. In my own child-hood, a century after Laurier's time, I knew people who spoke impeccable French—with an English accent. It was a kind of snobbery, a way of identifying oneself as a member of the dominant class, which had long been mainly English. In today's Quebec, it is considered a reflex of the colonized. This ignores the fact that many members of the French-speaking elite of the nineteenth century, including ardent nationalists such as Louis-Joseph Papineau, felt great admiration for the British and for the parliamentary democracy and economic prosperity they had brought to the province of Quebec. They found this political system far preferable to the atheistic and unstable republican system chosen by France—which, they remembered with bitterness, had "abandoned" their ancestors.

If Laurier's adversaries perceived his English accent—insofar as he actually had such an accent, since I have found no evidence of it—as a mark of disloyalty to the French "race," most French Canadians did not hold it against him, judging by his huge popularity.

AN ERROR OF YOUTH

During Laurier's youth, fierce debate was taking place in Lower Canada on the best way for French Canadians to survive in the United Canada that had resulted from the Durham Report. Should they resist with all their strength, as the great Papineau argued? Or should they, as the younger and pragmatic Louis-Hippolyte LaFontaine contended, seek allies among the English-speaking in order to obtain the responsible government for which the Patriotes had fought?

With the government of United Canada paralyzed by struggles between ideological and linguistic camps, the idea of a union of all the North American territories of the Crown began to gain ground. Negotiations in Charlottetown and Quebec City in 1864 led to a plan to form a confederation of the provinces of Quebec, Ontario, New Brunswick, and Nova Scotia. There was impassioned discussion of this new arrangement in Lower Canada. The Bleus, led by George-Étienne Cartier, favoured confederation, which would give French Canadians their own government for matters involving their culture (education, family, civil law), while the Rouges, led by Antoine-Aimé Dorion, were opposed to it, seeing it as a serious threat to the French language and the Catholic religion.

The role of the Catholic Church was another bone of contention in Lower Canada. Here again, the two camps were opposed. The Bleus had the support of most of the powerful bishops in French Canada; the Rouges called for the separation of church and state and the establishment of a public education system.

Wilfrid's father, Carolus, was a Rouge. So was Dr. Gauthier, with whom Wilfrid boarded while studying law in Montreal, and so was his mentor, Rodolphe Laflamme. Raised in liberalism, Laurier could only be a liberal. Therefore he was opposed to Confederation. From 1864 to 1867, when he was beginning his career as a lawyer, he participated actively in the movement against the union of the British colonies of America. He was part of a "national committee" of forty-six young professionals who felt that Confederation would be "detrimental to the interests of Lower Canada, would endanger its autonomy and would be a virtual renunciation of its most important right, the pure and simple recall of the current legislative Union."

In the fall of 1866, a few weeks before the politicians from the colonies were to meet in London to put the final touches on the confederation plan, Wilfrid was laid low by his worst attack of the mysterious ailment that dogged him. While working in his office on St. Gabriel Street, he collapsed, blood running from his mouth. This incident was a decisive event in his life. The leader of the Rouges, Antoine-Aimé Dorion, offered him the position of editor of *Le Défricheur*, the newspaper his recently deceased brother,

Jean-Baptiste-Éric, had founded in the village of L'Avenir in the Bois-Francs region. Wasn't the pure country air just what the frail Wilfrid needed?

So Laurier became editor of *Le Défricheur*. He used that platform to launch his final and fiercest salvoes against Confederation, faithful to the spirit of his fiery predecessor (who was nicknamed the "enfant terrible"): "Union is strength, yes, but only when the elements united are homogeneous. It will be in vain for you to throw together incongruous elements; there will be no strength, there will not even be union.... In this strange union every contrary element will meet face to face; the Catholic element and the Protestant element, the English element and the French element. From this moment there will be strife, war, anarchy; the weakest element, that is to say, the French and Catholic element, will be dragged along and swallowed up by the strongest."

Following the Rouge leaders, he criticized as excessive the powers accorded to the central government: "The project of Confederation binds us hand and foot to the English Colonies. We can do nothing, absolutely nothing. All important questions are within the sphere of the federal Government, that is to say, the Government of the English Colonies, and all the acts of our little local Parliament can be modified, corrected, cut, enlarged, annulled by the same Government."

What solution did he favour? This last passage is rarely quoted in English-language biographies of Laurier: "We have to return immediately and completely to Mr. Papineau's policy. To protest with all our strength against the new order of things that is being imposed on us and use the influence we still have to ask for and obtain a free and separate government."

Depending on the person's political views, this period of Laurier's life is interpreted either as an error of youth or as proof that Confederation was a mistake because at a particular time, Laurier himself took a dim view of it. For example, the historian Réal Bélanger writes: "How can we fail to appreciate the pertinence of certain other arguments concerning the domination of the minority by the majority? How, too, can we fail to remember the idea of the separation of Lower Canada, Laurier's ultimate solution?"

In contrast, Laurier LaPierre says in his hagiography of the man after whom he was named that even in his time, Laurier "was not an independentist." Laurier's first biographer, the journalist John Willison, felt that he was only following the editorial line established by Éric Dorion: "The spirit of the writing is that of *Le Défricheur* rather than that of Laurier." However, as Bélanger has shown, Laurier's texts in *Le Défricheur* were the culmination of many months of campaigning against Confederation, not isolated gestures. There is thus no doubt that at this time, Laurier, like all the Rouges, saw Confederation as a dangerous plan whose ultimate goal was the assimilation of the French Canadians. Nor is there any doubt that he saw the autonomy of Lower Canada ("a free and separate government") within the Empire as the last hope for French Canadians. Recognizing this in no way diminishes Laurier's subsequent achievements.

The fact remains that these writings against Confederation are surprising, because they are inconsistent with what we know about the young Laurier—his interest in and admiration for everything English, his words two years before at the graduation ceremony ("race hatreds are finished on our Canadian soil"), and what he said barely four years later in one of his first speeches in the Quebec Legislative Assembly: "It is a historical fact that the federation form was adopted only in order to maintain the exceptional and unique position of Quebec on the American continent."

Thus, there is in the period between 1864 and 1867 a paradoxical gap, a discontinuity. With Confederation achieved on July 1, 1867, Laurier's realistic, moderate, and conciliatory nature quickly became dominant again. While during the period of *Le Défricheur* he preferred the intransigence of Papineau to the pragmatism of LaFontaine ("good, generous, but cold and inexpressive"), when he became a politician he resolutely followed the path taken by the latter.

A MAN OF HIS WORD

After practising law for a few years, Laurier went into politics. He was elected to the Legislative Assembly of the province of Quebec in 1871. He was thirty years old, and Canada was four. You could say the country barely existed—or rather, it existed only on paper, in the form of the British North America Act, a dry document that offered no vision or inspiration for the new country. This union of colonies was the result not of the people's will, but of the dreams and aspirations of a few politicians and businessmen and the contract they had signed.

Wilfrid Laurier would owe his extraordinary career primarily to his prowess as a speaker. He was not the kind who fired up crowds—at that time, there was no lack of politicians with a gift for demagoguery. Laurier was different. He appealed to his listeners' emotions, certainly, but above all, to their intelligence. He reasoned with them, quoted authors, talked about history, and referred to precedents. He avoided insulting his adversaries and instead referred to the most noble ideals and values. His speeches were as upright as the man delivering them. He was sparing with gestures, but the ones he used expressed nobility, wisdom, and depth.

Some people are critical of the emphasis placed on the art of public speaking in politics and the media. However, in Laurier's time, as in our own, nothing is more important. The ability to convince, to move a crowd, is not in itself sufficient, but it is essential. In order to take action, politicians need to be able to win public support. To gain acceptance for difficult decisions, they must persuade people to reject the easy path and make sacrifices. To counter prejudices and heal wounds, they have to appeal to the highest human sentiments. This is why most of the great political leaders, from Lincoln to Obama, from Macdonald to Trudeau, have been exceptional orators. And Wilfrid Laurier was one. French Canadians were justly proud of Laurier's noble style and erudition: finally, one of their own was showing that he was equal to the anglophones, and was able to succeed not only in the province but on the vast scale of the new country.

The young member attracted notice with his first speech in the Legislative Assembly. In his response to the throne speech of Pierre-Joseph-Olivier Chauveau's Conservative government, Laurier talked about two subjects that would always be dear to him, the inadequacy of the province's education system and the fact that French Canadians lagged behind in industry. Unlike the clergy, Laurier did not feel that the future of his people lay in farming the land and cultivating religious faith. French-speaking Canadians, he maintained, should follow the example of their English-speaking neighbours: "We are surrounded by a strong and vigorous race who are endowed with a devouring activity and have taken possession of the entire universe as their field of labour. As a French-Canadian, I am pained to see my people eternally excelled by our fellow-countrymen of British origin. We must frankly acknowledge that down to the present we have been left behind in the race. We can admit this and admit it without shame, because the fact is explained by purely political reasons which denote no inferiority on our part. After the Conquest, the French-Canadians, desirous of maintaining their national inheritance intact, fell back upon themselves, and kept up no relations with the outside world." To Laurier, it was time for French Canadians to give up this policy of entrenchment and take their place in the modern world the British had built.

In this same speech, Laurier distanced himself forever from the navel-gazing of some of the clerical and nationalist elites of Quebec. "My patriotism will consist rather in telling my country the hard truths which will waken it from its lethargy and make it enter at last into the true way of progress and prosperity." This first speech in the assembly, however, was more striking for its tone, for being less partisan than the average, and for the dignified way in which it was delivered rather than for its content. The young member impressed his parliamentary colleagues and the journalists.

Moving to federal politics in 1874, Laurier was elected to the House of Commons as the member for Drummond-Arthabaska, part of the Liberal majority led by Alexander Mackenzie that would govern the country for a four-year interlude in John A. Macdonald's reign. Laurier made his first speech in the Commons in French, and a few weeks later, his first address in the language of the majority. The subject of that speech was extremely sensitive: whether Parliament should expel the rebel Louis Riel, who had just been elected to the House. A few years earlier, the rebellion of the Red River Métis in Manitoba had aroused strong emotions. For the first time since Confederation, francophones and anglophones were diametrically opposed. The English-speaking wanted the head of the man whose "provisional government" had shot one of their own, the

Orangeman Thomas Scott, during the uprising; they conveniently forgot the abuses committed against the Métis by English settlers in the North-West. The French Canadians spontaneously sympathized with Riel, a francophone; they closed their eyes to the arbitrary justice of which Scott had been the victim.

Tensions in the Commons were very high. But while the majority of the members gave in to their emotions, Laurier made a stirring appeal to reason and justice. As a French Canadian, he could have responded to the Riel affair by taking the easy path of following cultural prejudices. Instead, he chose to be guided by universal principles. This would continue to be a feature of his original, moderate yet bold approach to relations between the two principal nations that make up Canada.

Two amendments were proposed to the motion to expel Riel. The first one, which declared an amnesty for him, was the one clearly favoured by the francophones. Laurier spoke in defence of the other amendment, which stated that no decision would be made until a Commons committee had studied the matter. This, too, was typical of Laurier: rather than taking a firm position on a question, he generally tried to play for time. The elevated tone of his speeches gave the impression that he was taking a strong position, but the elegance of his words often camouflaged great circumspection. What his adversaries criticized as weakness would be his most formidable tactical weapon. Many years later, in a book on his famous friend, Laurent-Olivier David wrote: "His nature and his character led him to rely, perhaps sometimes too much, on time and the unexpected to resolve difficulties, to put off taking decisive action, to play the patient role of Fabius, but he claimed that temporizing had served him very well." In short, Laurier used time as all great political and military strategists do.

At the beginning of this speech on the fate of Riel, Laurier established his position in a surprising way: "I wish to declare at the outset that I have no preconceived opinion on the question before us. I have no bias against the member from Provencher (Riel) individually, nor do I have a predisposition in his favour." Few Canadians, anglophone or francophone, could have shown such objectivity, or would have dared to. Laurier came to Riel's defence, not because the Métis leader was French-speaking and was fighting for the rights of his people against the English Canadians, but because his basic rights, his rights as a British subject, were being flouted. In this matter, Laurier maintained, the House was acting somewhat as a court. Riel had never been formally charged with Scott's murder. On the contrary, the federal government had considered him the leader of a legitimate authority, with whom Ottawa had negotiated the creation of the new province of Manitoba and the transfer of land to the Métis. As part of the negotiations, Riel had even been promised that there would be no charges against him for acts committed during the uprising. How could Parliament now treat him like a fugitive from justice? "It may be argued, perhaps, that the reasons which I advance are pure legal subtleties," said Laurier. "Name them as you please, technical expressions, legal subtleties, it matters little: for my part, I say that these technical reasons, these legal subtleties, are the guarantees of British liberty. Thanks to these technical expressions, these legal subtleties, no person on British soil can be arbitrarily deprived of what belongs to him.... Since the days of the Great Charter, never has it been possible on British soil to rob a man of his liberty, his property or his honour except under the safeguard of what has been termed in this debate technical expressions and legal subtleties."

And what did Laurier say to his French Canadian compatriots who supported Métis leader unconditionally? Was he not in favour of amnesty? Of course. However, he felt that the strategy of the francophone members of Parliament was wrong and that the demand that the House decree an immediate amnesty would certainly be defeated. This practical sense of politics, which Laurier showed throughout his career, did not prevent him from defending Riel with conviction: "It has been said that Mr. Riel was only a rebel. How is it possible to use such language? What act of rebellion did he commit? Did he ever raise any other standard than the national flag? Did he ever proclaim any other authority than the sovereign authority of the Queen? No, never. His whole crime and the crime of his friends was that they wanted to be treated like British subjects and not bartered away like common cattle. If that be an act of rebellion, where is the one amongst us who if he had happened to have been with them would not have been rebels as they were? Taken all in all, I would regard the events at Red River in 1869–70 as constituting a glorious page in our history, if unfortunately they had not been stained with the blood of Thomas Scott. But such is the state of human nature and of all that is human: good and evil are constantly intermingled; the most glorious cause is not free from impurity and the vilest may have its noble side."

Over the years, Laurier often used this strategy: defending a cause dear to the French speakers of the country, he would try to win over the other "race" by appealing to principles that were dear to them, such as fair play and the rule of law. He wanted every cause to be judged on its merits, and not on the basis of language, religion, or ethnicity. Quite a demand! But isn't this the only attitude that is appropriate in an authentic democracy, in a society governed by the rule of law? Isn't it still the only one possible today, in a country as big and diverse as ours?

While he urged anglophones to remain faithful to the ideals of their mother country, Laurier asked francophones to understand that as a federal politician, he had to take into account the interests of everyone in the country. "I ask you one thing," he would say to Quebecers in his first public address as leader of the Liberal Party in 1887, "that, while remembering that I, a French-Canadian, have been elected leader of the Liberal Party of Canada, you will not lose sight of the fact that the limits of our common country are not confined to the province of Québec, but that they extend to all the territory of Canada, and that our country is wherever the British flag waves in America. I ask you to remember this in order to remind you that your duty is simply and above all to be Canadians."

The new member of Parliament impressed his colleagues and journalists from English Canada with his speech on Riel and his original, courageous approach to this explosive issue. The *Montreal Herald* commented: "Mr. Laurier made a magnificent speech in support of Mr. Holton's amendment. It may be the best of the whole debate—calm, logical, and thoughtful. He has made his mark and placed himself in the front rank of our debaters."

However, Laurier was not able to convince the majority of members of Parliament, and Riel was expelled from the House. The following year, the Mackenzie government offered Riel amnesty on condition that he leave the country for five years. Laurier supported this even though the people of Quebec would have preferred a full amnesty. In his view, a conditional amnesty was simply the best compromise possible.

Compromise is the key to Laurier's entire career as a public figure. Like most great Canadian leaders, he was a conciliator. He liked to quote the eighteenth-century Irish philosopher Edmund Burke: "All government, indeed every human benefit and enjoyment, every virtue and every prudent act is founded on compromise." It is this art of finding a middle course that would enable Laurier to govern the country so successfully for so many years. It is this art, too, that would earn him the enmity of radicals of every persuasion. To those who are blinded by an ideology, any compromise is a capitulation to evil. To those who fear the disappearance of their culture, it is the first step toward decline and extinction. Both the former and the latter see anyone who makes compromises as a weakling, an opportunist, or a traitor.

Dictionaries generally give two meanings for the word *compromise:* "a settlement of differences by mutual concessions" and "an act prejudicial to one's conscience." The two are not the same. A just compromise is one by which a person reaches an agreement with both his or her conscience and another party. In Latin, *compromissum* means "mutual agreement." Compromise is essential for individuals and countries. Without compromise, there is no marriage, no social life, no federalism—and no Canada. And those people, past and present, who have sought and worked out compromises should be seen not as weak, much less as traitors, but as the builders of our country.

THE GENTLEMAN

One might think that with his broad culture, his upright bearing, his natural nobility, and his rapid rise, Laurier would have put people off or that they would have found him haughty and cold. This was not at all the case. Everyone liked Laurier, even those who seriously disagreed with him. It is hard to say what made him so endearing. The man was certainly a model of politeness. Anyone who wrote him a letter received a detailed reply, and often an invitation to discuss the matter further in person. Those who quarrelled with him were treated with indulgence and usually returned the courtesy. One of them, the journalist John Willison, wrote that "with Laurier political separation was not followed by complete personal estrangement. The Liberal leader neither cherished resentments nor pursued vendettas." It was a remarkable character trait in the cut-throat world of politics, where disagreements are often perceived as attacks or betrayals, never forgiven and never forgotten.

Although Laurier was happiest when he was alone, reading, he loved the company of other people. He was interested in them, and curious about everything. He was the opposite of so many politicians, then and now, who like people only as an audience. At the same time, there was no excessive familiarity, no slaps on the back, no feigned friendship. Those who met him were not intimidated, yet always maintained a respectful distance.

And he loved books. He read constantly, everything from light novels to political biographies to legal treatises. In the photographs that remain of his offices on Parliament Hill and in his house in Ottawa, we see books covering the walls, the tables, and the desk. Today that house is a museum,

Laurier House, with a library of a few dozen of the books that belonged to him, bequeathed by his family. Among them are *A Report on Canada*, the famous and disastrous Durham Report; many books on the history of Canada; biographies of Lincoln, Danton, and Saint Francis of Assisi; *Que devons-nous à l'Angleterre?* written in 1915 by his great rival, the nationalist journalist and politician Henri Bourassa; French-Canadian novels such as *Le chercheur de trésors*, by Philippe Aubert de Gaspé, Jr., and *Jean Rivard, le défricheur*, by Antoine Gérin-Lajoie. Laurier read everything he got his hands on.

Few of his contemporaries would have thought that this scholar, this orator, who seemed too likeable, too naïve, and too fragile for politics would one day become leader of the Liberal Party and, a few years later, prime minister. As a member of Parliament in Ottawa, he seemed perfectly happy as the assistant and confidant of Alexander Mackenzie's successor as leader of the Liberal party, the brilliant, proud Edward Blake. In Parliament, he cultivated a reputation as indolent, spending more time in the library than in the smoky corridors where strategies were hatched and ambitions displayed. Laurier did not for a second see himself as Blake's successor; when Blake spoke of resigning, the member for Quebec-East was the first to try to dissuade him. The journalist J.W. Dafoe, who met him around this time, wrote: "He was then in his forty-third year, but in the judgment of many his career was over. His interest in politics was, apparently, of the slightest."

In 1887, after a second defeat by the elderly John A. Macdonald, Edward Blake gave up the leadership of the party. Had there been a spontaneous vote among the members of the Liberal caucus, Laurier would certainly not have been at the top of the list of potential successors. However, at that time, the influence of the outgoing leader was decisive. There was no doubt in Blake's mind that his faithful lieutenant Laurier should succeed him. Not only did Blake admire Laurier's personal qualities; he was convinced that the success of the Liberal Party depended on Quebec and that a French Canadian leader would be in the best position to win the province over to the Liberals.

The caucus approved this choice, without much enthusiasm, at a meeting on June 7. But Laurier hesitated for political and personal reasons. Politically, he did not see how a French-speaking Catholic leader could survive the attack of the Orangemen of Ontario, who were already displeased with his support for Riel and were beginning their crusade to abolish French and Catholic instruction in schools in all the provinces of Canada except Quebec. In personal terms, as he explained to his friend the lawyer and journalist Ernest Pacaud, "I lack fortune, I lack health.... I would very much like to fulfill my duty to my friends, but my friends are imposing too heavy a task on me."

Finally, Laurier gave in. His nomination was announced on June 23, the day before the feast day of St. John the Baptist, the patron saint of French Canadians.

ZOÉ AND ÉMILIE

Like Laurier's political life, his private life was full of contra-dictions. His strange relationship with Émilie Lavergne is the most remarkable example. Canadians of his time and since have been fascinated with this relationship, which was said to be "the romance of the century." Each of Laurier's biographers has taken a different position: some (such as amateur historian Charles Fisher) are convinced that the relationship was consummated, while others (the majority) maintain just as categorically that "sex didn't enter into their relationship" (Laurier LaPierre). As for me, I find nothing in the established facts or the documents available that would allow any firm conclusion on the precise nature of their relationship.

Wilfrid met his future wife, Zoé Lafontaine, when he arrived in Montreal in 1861. As mentioned above, he lived in the home of Dr. Séraphin Gauthier while studying law at McGill. Zoé also boarded there, with her mother. She was twenty years old, as he was, and she gave piano lessons. Demure and gentle, Zoé charmed Wilfrid. After he left Montreal to practise law and journalism in the Bois-Francs region on the south shore of the Saint-Lawrence River, the two exchanged many love letters. But Laurier hesitated to commit himself, fearing that he might "carry in my breast a seed of death that no power in the world can root out." Zoé, resigned, gave in to pressure from family and friends and finally accepted a marriage proposal from another suitor, Pierre Valois, a medical student. But the prospect of this union only made her more unhappy. Often at night she wept. Learning of this, Dr. Gauthier took the bull by the horns. A few days before the ceremony, he summoned Wilfrid to him, convinced him that he was only suffering from bronchitis, and pushed him into Zoé's arms. They were married that very evening. History does not tell us how poor Pierre Valois, the fiancé who was abandoned at the altar, reacted.

This episode led Charles Fisher to conclude that Laurier's "marriage to Zoé Lafontaine was no more than the yielding of an emotionally immature, sick young man, to pressure from Zoé's mother, and from Dr. Gauthier and his wife in

Montréal." I do not see what basis Fisher has for this statement. All indications are, on the contrary, that the two young people were very much in love. One thing is certain—their love blossomed and it aged well. Only Wilfrid's death, after fifty years of life together, would separate the couple.

Laurier became friends with Émilie Barthe in 1876 in Arthabaskaville, where he had moved after short stays in L'Avenir and Victoriaville. He was thirty-five years old and she was twenty-seven. She had just married Wilfrid's associate and friend Joseph Lavergne. The daughter of a prominent citizen, she had lived for a time in Paris as a child. Before coming to the Bois-Francs, she lived in Detroit. In short, her horizons were much broader than those of the vast majority of French Canadians of the time. Not particularly pretty, but a real fashion plate, a great reader, and, especially, a great talker, Émilie left no one indifferent. Her love of books and conversation, her anglophilia, and her class attracted Laurier. He developed the habit of leaving the office for an hour or two, quite openly, to visit Émilie in her living room and discuss literature. That was enough to raise certain people's eyebrows.

Émilie gave birth to two children, Gabrielle (1877) and Armand (1880). People began to whisper that Armand looked a lot like Wilfrid Laurier (who had no children with Zoé). The rumour that Armand was his illegitimate son was spread by Laurier's Conservative adversaries. It never completely died out. Joseph Lavergne, Armand, and Émilie all swore that it was not true, but to no avail. "The resemblance is so striking!" some history buffs have told me.

I have in front of me photographs of Armand Lavergne and Wilfrid Laurier. The resemblance that has been so talked about does not appear obvious to me. There is the receding hairline, the curly hair, the aquiline nose. But Armand's chin is stronger. There is a rebellious expression in his eyes and mouth, while Laurier's express seriousness and gentleness. A person who believes that the young Lavergne carried Laurier's genes will find support for that position in these photos; someone who believes the opposite will be equally convinced.

It is clear, however, that Armand had both a close and difficult relationship with his parents' friend. Laurier took a great deal of interest in the young man and felt he had a promising future, but he was critical of Armand's laziness and his stubborn refusal to learn English. In 1904, Laurier recruited him as a candidate. Elected to the House of Commons, Armand was more attracted to the rationalist genius of nationalist Henri Bourassa than to the pragmatic politics of his mentor. The young member of Parliament was so critical of the policies of the government and caused so much trouble for the Liberals that the leader finally expelled him from the party in 1907. Lavergne went on to have a long career in provincial and federal politics. Elected in Quebec City as a nationalist, he later became a Conservative. He continued to fiercely denounce Laurier's policies, while asking him for favours for members of his family. The prime minister suffered a great deal as a result of this behaviour, which Armand attempted to explain in a letter sent on December 6, 1910: "Every time duty calls me loudly, the past whispers softly: 'Tu quoque Brute.' I must appear to you as an ingrate. As God is my witness, I love you; but, and please forgive me, I love my country more."

The theory of a love affair between Wilfrid Laurier and Émilie Lavergne was reinforced by the discovery of what some have called "love letters" he sent her between 1891 and 1893. Historian Marc La Terreur first published these letters in 1963. Charles Fisher acquired the originals in 1971 and published them, with annotations, in 1989. The two men drew contradictory conclusions on the nature of the relationship.

It is certainly true that Wilfrid's letters to Émilie expressed great mutual trust, feelings of intimacy, and even passion. Some passages are frankly disturbing. Some examples:

"I would wish for a long rest. Could I join you & spend a few days of sun & breeze in your company? I would come back as strong as Samson. You would find me a very dull companion the first days, & rather exacting. I would compel you to talk, & to talk all the time. All this is a dream, impossible to attain, & still pleasant to indulge in." A long rest in Émilie's company? What about Zoé? In these forty letters, Laurier does not once mention his wife, whom Émilie saw regularly in Arthabaskaville.

"It is true my dear friend, you never sang for me; that is one of the sacrifices of life. How often I have pictured to myself, that I was sitting by your piano, listening to your voice. I heard you once, last summer. From the open window of my room, I heard your voice, faint it is true from the distance, still audible. My heart was big that night, & the words went deep into my heart, though I could hardly then respond to the sentiment which they gave expression to (it was the barcarolle song by Coquelin). All the emotions which that voice evoked, are still as fresh in my soul as they were these thirteen months ago." Let us recall that it was when he heard Zoé play the piano some thirty years earlier that Wilfrid had fallen in love with her.

The form of these letters contributes to the mystery. They are almost all written in English, while Émilie's letters, now lost, were apparently written in French. They are dated only with the number of the day, without any indication of the year or the month. Émilie's name is never mentioned, only "my dear friend." The people discussed are identified only by the initials of their first names. Each letter is signed W.L. It is as if Laurier was on his guard and was trying to cover his tracks. Unless it was simply a game between the two friends—a rather childish game for a man of fifty and a woman in her forties.

It should be said that in all his writings, as always in his politics, Laurier was a very cautious man. The person to whom he entrusted his official correspondence, the academic Oscar D. Skelton, stated: "Sir Wilfrid's caution and his remarkable memory lessened the extent to which he committed himself on paper. He never wrote a letter when he could hold a conversation, and never filed a document when he could store the fact in his memory."

Two of the letters to Mme Lavergne show that Laurier was concerned about what would happen if someone found out about this exchange. When Émilie was staying in Murray Bay, where the former Liberal leader Edward Blake was as well, Wilfrid ordered her, "under no circumstances, &

for no reason, never show him a letter from me." Later, he told Émilie that he had received a letter that had been opened and that other pieces of mail had arrived very late: "Even if there are in a letter only things which the whole world could read you must admit that there is nothing more exasperating than this conviction that the secret of your correspondence is no longer secure."

Some passages, on the other hand, express the disgust that lechery inspired in Laurier. He wrote of Louis XV and the Marquise de Pompadour (in French, this time): "In Louis XV, there was only sensuality; in her, there was only intrigue." About Joséphine, he said, "She was an inveterate coquette, & had I been in Napoléon's place, I would have been unmerciful." He said of his good friend Ernest Pacaud, who was caught up in a political and financial scandal, "He must learn the lesson that after all there is such a thing as chastity among women & honor among men, that human actions can have another inspiration than selfishness or vile appetites." It is hard to imagine these words coming from the pen of an adulterous man writing to his mistress.

It is also interesting to compare these letters to Émilie Lavergne with Laurier's letters to Zoé that have come down to us. Some fifty of them, most written between 1867 and

1879—that is, in the months preceding their marriage and the eleven following years—are in the possession of Library and Archives Canada. This correspondence thus predates the famous "love letters" by more than a decade.

Like the letters to Émilie, those written to Zoé begin with "My dear friend," except for the ones written before their marriage, which begin with "My dear, good Zoé." The letters to Zoé are signed "Your friend, Wilfrid," while those to Émilie, as we saw, are signed "W.L."

After their marriage, Laurier's letters to Zoé are usually more down to earth than those he would write to Émilie. He never writes about books in them (except once, about a gardening book). He rarely discusses his feelings, other than his boredom in Quebec City and later in Ottawa. He often informs her that he will have to delay his return to Arthabaskaville because the session has been extended or he has to take part in a trial in some distant part of the province. The couple speak of their cats as if they were their children; they are, as Laurier says, "our little family." Another topic was the couple's finances.

It is surprising, in view of Laurier's deep involvement in politics from 1874 until the end of his days, that he talks so little about it with the two women in his life. In his messages to both Zoé and Émilie, he makes only brief allusions to it.

He even seems happy to deal with lighter matters such as the behaviour of a cat or the life of Madame de Staël. Perhaps, too, like most men of his time, he felt that public affairs were not the business of women.

We note, finally, that Wilfrid does not hesitate to tell Zoé he loves her and that he gives her "a thousand kisses," words we do not find in his correspondence with Émilie, where there is never any mention of love or physical contact of any kind, past, hoped for, or dreamed of. This suggests that while their relationship may have been very strong, even passionate, it remained at the level of fantasy.

In any case, for more than twenty years, Émilie played an important role in Laurier's life. After he became prime minister, he appointed Joseph Lavergne judge of the Superior Court of the District of Ottawa; according to the gossip, this was a way of bringing Émilie closer to him. At this time, Émilie was often seen with the Lauriers at society functions. She even helped Zoé set up the couple's new household on Theodore Street (now called Laurier Street). She taught them about the ways of the world, since she was comfortable in high society, whereas Wilfrid, and especially Zoé, were still novices in these matters. But Laurier was no fool, and he quickly learned how to conduct himself during the many receptions he was invited to.

We should thus be skeptical of the claim Mme Lavergne made many years later that she had been responsible for Laurier's education: "I taught him to eat, to dress with taste, in a word, all that a gentleman should know."

Without anyone knowing exactly why (historians suppose that it was to protect his political career), Laurier suddenly decided to distance himself from Émilie. At some point in his first term as prime minister, he returned the letters she had written to him. Their correspondence became more sporadic and less intimate. During the same period, Laurier transferred Joseph to the Superior Court of Montreal. When the position of chief justice of the Court of King's Bench of the province of Quebec opened up, Émilie and Armand felt it should go to Joseph and never doubted that the prime minister would appoint him. Instead, Laurier named Sir Louis-Amable Jetté, earning him the resentment of the Lavergnes. With Émilie kept at a distance, Zoé played her role as wife of the prime minister with increasing skill. Everyone praised her kindness, her modesty, and her efficiency.

Let us briefly go back in time. On November 20, 1875, Laurier had just turned thirty-four. His destiny had been joined with that of Zoé Lafontaine for seven years. In his room in Ottawa, he wrote to her, "Thank God, [these seven years] have passed without a cloud, you have always been good and devoted." Many clouds subsequently darkened the sky, and Laurier's relationship with Émilie Lavergne must have been the heaviest of them. But Zoé remained steadfastly at her husband's side. Much has been said of the influence Émilie supposedly had on Laurier; we too often forget that he would not have become what he was without the care and unshakable support of that "dear, good Zoé."

CHAPTER 2

The "Races"

> Confederation will be the tomb of the French race and the
> ruin of Lower Canada.
> **WILFRID LAURIER, 1866**

> The governing motive of my life has been to harmonize the
> diverse elements which compose our country. I cannot say
> yet if I have been as successful as I would have wanted and
> as I would have hoped, but the thought is true, and in the
> end it will triumph.
> **WILFRID LAURIER, 1905**

In the early days following Confederation, two political
parties, the Conservatives and the Liberals, began their
domination of Canadian politics. The Conservative Party
was spurred on by its extremists. In English Canada, these
were the Orangemen, descendants of Protestants from
Ulster, whose most effective spokesman in Laurier's time was
the lawyer, gentleman farmer, and member of Parliament
D'Alton McCarthy. In French Canada, the Conservatives
were controlled by the ultramontanist Catholic clergy, who
felt that the church should oversee every aspect of society, in
particular education and government. In their view, "the

separation of Church and State is an absurd and impious doctrine" and "it is necessary that those who exercise the legislative authority be in full agreement with the teachings of the Church."

In the Liberal Party, the French Canadian Rouges and the Ontario Clear Grits, who were staunchly anticlerical, had been marginalized. The party was moderate, although its adversaries continued to associate it with its radical past.

In the province of Quebec, this period was marked by the growth of a new nationalism, led with brio by Henri Bourassa, grandson of the great Patriote leader Louis-Joseph Papineau. Bourassa was elected to the House of Commons as a Liberal in 1896, the same year Laurier became prime minister. Bourassa was as uncompromising as he was brilliant, and he soon found his leader too soft in his defence of the interests of French Canadians. Bourassa not only demanded that the autonomy of the province of Quebec be protected; he also argued that Confederation was made up of two equal peoples, English and French. Francophones should therefore have the same rights as anglophones throughout the country, in particular the right to send their children to separate Catholic French-language schools. At that time, the idea of a country made up of two nations with equal rights from sea to sea was new. This was not the view of the French Canadian proponents of Confederation, who above all had wanted francophones to have control over their own affairs in the province of Quebec. As for most English-speaking politicians, to them, aside from the province of Quebec, Canada was destined to be an English country.

There was heated debate between these different groups, for good reason: the very nature of the young country was at stake. Would Canada remain a colony of the United Kingdom or would it one day be an independent country? Would it be Protestant, Catholic, or both? Would it resist the attraction of its neighbour to the south, which was becoming more and more powerful?

The Orangemen were fanatical imperialists and anti–French Canadian. In their view, Canada had to serve the interests of the British Empire. There was no doubt in their minds about the superiority of English culture and the Protestant religion, so Canada had to be English and Protestant. D'Alton McCarthy wanted to achieve no less than the assimilation of the French Canadians as proposed by Durham a half-century earlier: "This is a British country, and the sooner we take in hand our French Canadian fellow subjects and make them British in sentiment and teach them the English language, the less trouble we shall have to prevent. Sooner or later it must be settled." He even alluded to the possibility of accomplishing this by force of arms. There ensued a series of manoeuvres aimed at doing away with all teaching of the Catholic religion and the French language in the territories and provinces outside Quebec. Not all the supporters of the Empire were so closed-minded, but as so often occurs in politics, the voices of the radicals drowned out those of the moderates.

The nationalists in Quebec resisted with religious zeal any policy they saw as weakening the rights of francophones and Catholics (Bourassa himself was very devout). Even for the regions of the country where Catholic francophones were a tiny minority and the struggle was essentially theoretical, they rejected any change to the laws and regulations, any compromise. Bourassa declared, "There can be no conciliation between justice and injustice."

The Quebec nationalists were also fiercely opposed to imperialism, and felt that Canada should become as independent as possible from England. In particular, they thought that Canadians should be free to decide whether to participate in wars sparked by London's imperial ambitions. Thus, paradoxically, Bourassa's supporters were among the pioneers of Canadian nationalism. However, to the dismay of its founder, this movement gradually became attached solely to the territory of Quebec. Eventually it turned into a quest for political independence.

By nature, Wilfrid Laurier was the opposite of an extremist. Throughout his career, he was constantly caught in the crossfire between the Orangemen, the ultramontanists, and the nationalists. To those who dreamed of eradicating the French language from Canada, he replied by appealing to the values at the heart of British democracy: "I denounce this policy as anti-Canadian; I denounce it as anti-British; I denounce it as being at variance with all the traditions of British government in this country." This was a brilliant strategy, showing the Orangemen's contradiction with the principles of which they claimed to be the greatest defenders.

To the rejection of compromise by Bourassa and the French Canadian Catholic Church, Laurier responded with a call for realism. Francophones certainly had to preserve their rights, but they must not get caught up in futile battles. Since Confederation was in the interest of French Canadians—without it, they would be absorbed by the United States—and since they were in the minority, taking a hard line would be suicidal. Six months before his death, despite all the crises he had experienced, all the defeats he had suffered, Laurier remained convinced of the virtues of harmonious relations between Canadians of British and

French origins: "There were among us narrow-minded people who shouted, 'No compromise; all or nothing.' How absurd! When a minority declares that it will concede nothing, that it will demand everything and will accept nothing less, there is none so blind as he who does not see that the inevitable result will be: nothing. How can one not see that the majority will itself accept that doctrine, and will apply it without remorse to those who proclaim it!"

Laurier was a practical man, and his adversaries were ideologues. The imperialists wanted a Canada in the image and in the service of England; they failed to understand that this would lead to the breakup of the country. Bourassa wanted a bilingual Canada that was as autonomous as possible from the United Kingdom; he failed to realize he could not flout the views of the English Protestant majority. Laurier dreamed of a united Canada, loyal to the Empire but moving slowly and surely toward greater autonomy, where the French language and the Catholic religion would *as far as possible* be preserved. His objectives as leader were the unity of Canada, the unity of the Liberal Party, and power, and he saw them as interdependent.

An admirer of Abraham Lincoln, Laurier adopted the American president's principle of government that no cause, even the most noble, was higher than the survival of the nation. Let us recall Lincoln's famous letter to the editor of the *New York Tribune*, Horace Greeley: "My paramount object in this struggle is to save the Union, and is not either to save or to destroy slavery. If I could save the Union without freeing any slave I would do it; and if I could save it by freeing some and leaving others alone I would also do that." Laurier took from this the lesson that "in a democracy such as ours, American or English, we must study and measure public opinion, and in this way it is possible to guide it while indulging it." He added: "The principles are immutable, but their application is infinitely varied."

Those who are seeking a knight in shining armour, a defender of principles against all odds, will be disappointed by Wilfrid Laurier. Those who know that a man of principle can govern only by showing patience and realism will find in him a model.

"I AM A FRENCH CANADIAN"

Like every French Canadian who has fought for understanding between the country's anglophones and francophones, Laurier was accused by some of his own people of being a traitor, of colluding with "the enemy," of "selling out." Among other things, they criticized his English accent and the admiration he so often expressed for British culture and institutions. Does this mean Laurier did not love his people or that he looked down on them? Wasn't there contempt in his famous reply to Bourassa, who asked him if he paid attention to Quebec's opinion on the Boer War: "My dear Henri, the province of Quebec has no opinions, it only has feelings"?

This is not the case. Laurier knew and loved French Canadians as much as anyone did. He loved them enough to see their weaknesses and state them. For example, in a letter to the young lawyer Léon-Mercier Gouin, he commented on Louis Hémon's novel, *Maria Chapdelaine*, which was published in 1913, criticizing the bleak picture the French writer had drawn of the colonists and that they themselves liked to present: "All these pioneers, it is true, love to dwell on the obstacles they have to surmount and to exaggerate the rudeness of their lives. Odilon Desbois, a settler whom I knew very well in Arthabaska, said one day in my presence: 'I am on the eleventh range of Trigwick, far from bread, behind the meat.' That is the invariable story of our people; they are pleased to cry poverty and famine. Hémon should have remembered that 'the Frenchman born a grouser' remains a grouser."

Laurier was actually very proud of his origins. He cultivated his mother tongue that was "so rich, so flexible, so malleable that, in the hands of a master who knows how to use it, there is no musical instrument that compares to it for variety and harmony." He declared with feeling to a hostile audience in Toronto in 1886: "I honour and esteem English institutions. I do not regret that we are now subjects of the Queen instead of Canada; but may my right hand wither by my side if the memories of my forefathers ever cease to be dear to my ears." And three years later, in the same city, he said: "I am a French-Canadian; I was brought up on the knees of a French mother, and my first recollections are those recollections which no man ever forgets. And shall it be denied to me, the privilege of addressing the same language to those who are dear to me?"

He was as much a connoisseur of French culture as of English. He said he was a follower of the English politician William Gladstone, but also of the liberal priest Henri Lacordaire. During his first voyage to France, he quoted Victor Hugo to explain to his audience the dual attachment he felt to his mother country and to England: "'True to the double blood that was poured into my veins by my father, an old soldier, and my mother, a Vendean.'"

As we have seen, Laurier was profoundly convinced that French Canadians, given their minority status, had nothing to gain by being intransigent in struggles that could only be suicidal. Above all, he believed that it was up to them to take their rightful place rather than expecting English Canadians to give it to them. "To me," he wrote to Conservative member of Parliament Charles Angers in 1896, "the salvation of the French race is not in isolation, but in struggle. Let us give our children the best education possible, let us put them on an equal footing with those of the other race, and let us give them the legitimate pride they will feel in such a struggle. That way lies salvation. That way lies autonomy." "What attitude, tell me, should French Canadians adopt in the Confederation?" he asked Bourassa. "They have to either isolate themselves, to go their own way, or march at the head of Confederation. They have to choose between British imperialism and American imperialism. I see no other alternative."

Laurier was also convinced that Canadian nationhood would be built not on the ruins of the old "races," but with these groups as its pillars: "We are Canadians," he declared. "Below the island of Montreal the water that comes from the North, the Ottawa, unites with the waters that come from the Western lakes, but uniting they do not mix. There they run parallel, separate, distinguishable, and yet are one stream, flowing within the same banks, the mighty Saint-Lawrence, rolling on toward the sea bearing the commerce of a nation upon its bosom—a perfect image of our nation."

"Our country is not confined to the territory overshadowed by the Citadelle of Québec; our country is Canada," he said in a speech he gave on Saint-Jean-Baptiste Day in 1889. "Our fellow-countrymen are not only those in whose veins runs the blood of Canada. They are all those, whatever their race or whatever their language, whom the fortune of war, the chances of fate, or their own choice have brought among us and who acknowledge the sovereignty of the British Crown. The rights of my fellow-countrymen are as dear to me, as sacred to me, as the rights of my own race. What I claim for ourselves is an equal place in the sun, an equal share of justice, of liberty; that share we have, and what we claim for ourselves we are anxious to grant to others."

At this time, Laurier enjoyed the unswerving support of the majority of francophone Quebecers. In all the elections in which he led the Liberal forces, his party took a majority of the seats in his native province. He was practically worshipped. His photo hung on kitchen or living room walls in many homes. Senator Serge Joyal, an avid collector, has found all kinds of manufactured items with images of the great man—plates, snuff boxes, stained glass, and so on.

Mr. Joyal likes to say that Laurier was a pioneer of branding. Nationalist intellectuals, however, were hostile to Laurier. After the Liberal leader's death, they undertook to tarnish his reputation and replace him with Bourassa. Just as those former objects of veneration are now gathering dust in antique shops, Laurier's fame today is confined to old books on the shelves of public libraries.

RIEL AGAIN

The most important conflicts between the founding "races" of the country concerned the Métis rebellions in the North-West, the preservation of the education rights of francophone Catholics west of Quebec, and Canadians' participation in the Empire's wars.

I spoke above of the strong impression Laurier had made on members of Parliament and journalists in 1874 with his speech on the fate of Louis Riel after the Red River Rebellion. Twelve years later, he made an even more remarkable appeal with regard to Riel.

After the rebellion in Manitoba, the life of the Métis leader took many unexpected turns. He fled to the United States and took up residence there, returning to Canada secretly from time to time. During this period, a meeting took place about which, unfortunately, we know very little.

Laurier was invited by a priest in the Arthabaska region to meet an interesting individual. When he stepped into the presbytery, he found himself face to face with Louis Riel. Laurier's impression of the ensuing conversation, in which they discussed religion and politics—American and European—was that Riel "is a monomaniac. He hoisted upon himself [the role of] the prophet and liberator of the half-breeds," he wrote to Edward Blake.

As Laurier observed, Riel's mental state was unstable. His religious visions led him to spend two years in psychiatric hospitals in Montreal and then Beauport, near Quebec City. Then, having apparently learned to control his religious zeal, he went back to live in the United States. In the meantime, the guarantees given to the Métis when Manitoba was created had not solved their problems. Those who had taken refuge in the neighbouring territory of Saskatchewan once again saw their land and their way of life threatened by white settlement. Years went by, and the Conservative government turned a deaf ear to their petitions. Quite naturally, the Métis called upon the man who had led them to victory at Red River, and Louis Riel returned to Canada in 1884.

This second uprising, known as the North-West Rebellion, was put down after a few weeks, but its conclusion—the execution of Riel—remains one of the

most dramatic events in Canadian history. The Macdonald
government's refusal to commute his sentence enraged
French Canadians, and a huge rally took place in the Champ
de Mars in Montreal. This was one of the rare times in his
career that Laurier lost his temper: "Had I been born on the
banks of the Saskatchewan, I would myself have shouldered
a musket to fight against the neglect of governments and the
shameless greed of speculators." This uncharacteristic statement would be held against him for a long time. He would
not be caught saying such a thing again.

For months, the country was torn by this conflict, divided
once again on the basis of language. In Ontario, the press
railed against "French Canadian domination." The *Mail*
blustered, "After all our efforts to establish amicable relations
with them, even at the sacrifice of our prosperity, the French
Canadians are now seeking to compel us to recognize their
right to suspend the operation of the law whenever a representative of their race is in the toils." The storm also swept
through Parliament. Late in the evening of March 16, 1886,
when the exhausted members were nodding off or having a
drink in the antechamber, Wilfrid Laurier rose to his feet.
Knowing his talents as an orator, the MPs returned to their
seats. They were not disappointed.

Laurier first came to the defence of his people, the French

Canadians, against the racist attacks of the anglophone press. To the accusations of the *Mail* in particular, he answered firmly: "I denounce this as a vile calumny. I denounce this as false. I claim this for my fellow countrymen of French origin that there is not to be found anywhere, under heaven, a more docile, quiet and law-abiding people."

Then, producing documents in his support like a Crown attorney in a trial, he accused the government of responsibility for Louis Riel's death. It was a brilliant speech, passionate and unflinching. The apathy of the government had led only to blood, he declared: "Blood, blood, blood! Prisons, scaffolds, widows, orphans, destitution, ruin, these are what fill the blank in the administration of this government of the affairs of the North-West!"

Does not a government have a duty to suppress rebellion? he asked rhetorically. Of course. However, he added: "Rebellion is always an evil, it is always an offence against the positive law of a nation; it is not always a moral crime.… What is hateful is not rebellion but the despotism which induces that rebellion; what is hateful are not rebels but the men who, having the enjoyment of power, do not discharge the duties of power."

The rebellion had to be stopped. But once that was accomplished, given the legitimacy of the rebels' motives, the government owed them clemency. Riel himself was doubly entitled to clemency, because despite what the government's doctors said, he was clearly not of sound mind: "I am not of those who look upon Louis Riel as a hero.... At his worst he was a subject fit for asylum; at his best he was a religious and political monomaniac."

Laurier then demonstrated that Riel's trial had been unfair. Finally, he disputed the reasons given by the Conservatives to justify the Métis's execution, stating that they had hanged him not because of the recent rebellion, but to avenge the murder of Thomas Scott during the Red River Rebellion. In other words, it was purely a political act, and thus all the more irresponsible: "I ask any man on the other side of the House, if this offence was punishable then, why was it not punished then, and if it was not punishable, why is it punished now? This issue of the death of Thomas Scott has long been buried, and now it is raised by whom? It is raised by members opposite, the last men who should ever speak of it. Sir, we are a new nation, we are attempting to unite the different conflicting elements which we have into a nation. Shall we ever succeed if the bond of union is to be revenge?"

Laurier's words were so powerful that the MPs were stunned. He took his seat, and the House adjourned. It was ten after midnight. The next day, the Liberal leader, Edward

Blake, described the speech by his Quebec lieutenant as "the finest parliamentary speech ever pronounced in the Parliament of Canada since Confederation." Even the Conservatives expressed admiration. The minister of the interior, Thomas White, declared: "It is a matter of common pride to us that any public man in Canada can make, on the floor of Parliament, such a speech as we listened to last night."

After this speech the press would describe Wilfrid Laurier as "silver tongued."

THE SCHOOLS

During Laurier's career, there were repeated conflicts around the education rights of Catholic francophones living outside Quebec. As leader of the Liberal Party, he had to deal with this issue on at least five separate occasions:

- D'Alton McCarthy's motion in the House of Commons proposing the withdrawal of French's official status in the North-West Territories and stating that "there should be community of language among the people of Canada" (1890),
- the laws of the Manitoba government aimed at abolishing separate (Catholic) schools in that province (1890),

- the Autonomy Bills creating the provinces of Saskatchewan and Alberta (1905),
- the law adding part of the District of Keewatin, in the north, to the territory of Manitoba (1912), and
- Regulation 17, adopted by the Ontario government, limiting the teaching of French in the schools of the province (1913).

The political circumstances and local situations differed from one conflict to another, but in each case, Laurier had to react to attempts to limit the rights of francophone Catholics in the country, in particular the right of French Canadians in the English-speaking provinces to send their children to separate schools. The justifications for these proposed policies varied from the most reasonable—to improve the quality of education in the schools, to standardize the provincial education system—to the most despicable—to erase any trace of Catholicism or French from the country. They invariably drew a vehement reaction from the Catholic clergy and the francophone population of Quebec, Laurier's political base. These debates were marked by enormous demagoguery and intolerance, especially on the anglophone side, where the Orange Order was at its height.

During this quarter-century of conflicts, Laurier

maintained essentially the same position. This consistency was based both on principles and on a profound spirit of conciliation dictated by the need to preserve the unity of the country and of his party, and to win and hold on to power. Practicality also necessitated the quest for compromise, according to Laurier. What was of primary importance to him was the situation on the ground. Beyond legal quibbling, what was really happening in the schools? Were the students receiving Catholic religious instruction and a French education? How many were affected by a particular policy?

When, in 1890, Laurier stood up against McCarthy's motion, it was not out of sympathy for the francophones in the North-West, who were few in number (some five thousand) and—he said this openly—were not worth a national crisis, but because of what that motion presaged for Catholics and francophones throughout the country. The same was true twenty years later with respect to the education rights of a few francophones in Keewatin, for whom he refused to refight the battle of Manitoba. "It was above all a question of principle, since the population was very small," conceded the historian Robert Rumilly, a biographer and admirer of Henri Bourassa, regarding the Keewatin affair, hastening to add, "but a very high question of principle."

However, Laurier did not care about questions of principle, as high as they might be, if they did not have a significant practical (and political) impact.

This attitude does not make Laurier a crass opportunist. He approached the issue of education rights armed with certain solid convictions: the need to preserve the spirit of 1867, and in particular, to safeguard the Catholic and Protestant minorities; the protection of provincial autonomy; and the promotion of individual bilingualism, especially the learning of English by francophones.

THE SPIRIT OF 1867—Laurier felt that the country would collapse if Canadians did not allow themselves to be guided by the compromises made at the creation of the Confederation. This meant that linguistic and religious diversity had to be respected and preserved. "I need not remind you that upon many questions, Confederation was a compromise," he wrote in 1905 to J.R. Dougall, editor of the *Montreal Witness*. "The education clause of the B.N.A. Act was the most remarkable of all and in that clause George Brown, who was a most determined opponent of separate schools, agreed not only to admit the system in his own province, but to make its continuance part of the constitution.... I am well aware that the idea of having schools partaking of ecclesiastical domination is repugnant to the spirit of our age. Even such an objection could not hold against the spirit of the constitution."

Paradoxically, Laurier's nationalist adversaries in Quebec also demanded respect for the compromise of 1867. But their interpretation of that compromise was not the same as Laurier's. For Bourassa, as we saw above, the recognition of francophones' rights in federal institutions meant that the two founding peoples were equal, and therefore that the country "would be French and English in each of its parts as well as in its whole." Laurier also felt that Confederation confirmed the equality of the two "races," but to him, the concrete realization of that equality had to take into account certain facts, in particular demographic change. The rapid growth of the non-francophone population in the West since Confederation meant that French speakers now consti-tuted a very small minority (around 5 percent) in those huge territories. The immigration of people with various mother tongues increased the importance of establishing a common language—which, in these places, could only be English. Whatever idealists thought, a practising politician could not ignore that reality.

On the other side of the barricades, the Orangemen had a much narrower interpretation of the agreement of 1867.

They conceded that the French language and the Catholic religion had been granted a special status in Quebec and (with respect to Catholicism) in Ontario, but felt that this "folly" must not be repeated in the rest of the country, or else Canada, divided from sea to sea between two races, could not become a great nation. Drawing on the Durham Report, D'Alton McCarthy maintained that "there is no more important matter in the formation of the character of a people than the language that they speak." McCarthy denied that he harboured any hostility toward francophones: "My only desire is to promote the welfare of us all, and I think our truest interest will be found in trying to create and build up in this country one race with one national life, and with a language common to us all." Outside the House, however, McCarthy was less moderate, going so far as to call francophones a "bastard nationality." Laurier retorted: "Certainly no one can respect or admire more than I do the Anglo-Saxon race; I have never disguised my sentiments on that point, but we of French origin are satisfied to be what we are and we claim no more. I claim this for the race in which I was born that though it is not perhaps endowed with the same qualities as the Anglo-Saxon race, it is endowed with qualities as great; I claim for it that it is endowed with qualities unsurpassed in some respects; I claim for it that there is not today under the sun a more moral, more honest or more intellectual race." (D'Alton McCarthy's long and violent campaign against francophones would not prevent Laurier from considering him for appointment to his Cabinet in 1898. This was a brilliant tactical manoeuvre aimed at winning the electoral support of Orange sympathizers—but still, there are times when Laurier strikes even admirers as far too conciliatory!)

The Orangemen were not the only ones who wanted to diminish as much as possible the presence of the Catholic religion and the French language in the country. Many anglophone moderates held the view that the compromise of 1867 applied only to the provinces that existed at that time. One of these was the Manitoban Clifford Sifton, whom Laurier recruited to his first Cabinet. A leading figure in the provincial government of Thomas Greenway, Sifton did not see why Catholic francophones in Manitoba should be given the privilege of having separate schools when there were other linguistic and religious groups that were equally numerous. For example, there were fifteen thousand Mennonites in Manitoba, while Catholic French Canadians numbered twelve thousand.

Moreover, Sifton claimed—and all indications are that he was not wrong—that the Catholic schools in the province were of very poor quality: "One could go from one end of Manitoba to the other, and he would not find among the business or professional men a young man from any of those [French-speaking] families. The children of such families remained on the farm where they were born. There was no idea of progress among them. If this system were imposed upon them permanently it would simply make them hewers of wood and drawers of water." In other words, the clergy were doing no better a job of educating children in Manitoba than they were in Quebec, where liberals demanded that the state wrest control of the schools and colleges from the church. Reform was needed in the west as in the east. But did reform have to involve abolishing separate schools and French education outside the province of Quebec? Of course not. This was where prejudice overcame reason.

Laurier did not propose measures to favour French outside Quebec, but he opposed any policy aimed at depriving francophones of the means to preserve their language: "It was not intended that any [nationality] should give up its characteristic, but it was expected that though every nationality might retain its individuality, yet that all would be actuated by one aspiration and would endeavour to form one nation."

PROVINCIAL AUTONOMY—During this period, the autonomy of the provincial governments was one of the keystones of the Liberal Party's philosophy. It was hardly surprising, then, that Laurier was a proponent of this policy. For him, however, it was not merely a matter of endorsing the party line. He was convinced that provincial autonomy was essential to the country's survival, that it made it possible to preserve the diversity of Canada, since it allowed the provinces to adopt different policies corresponding to the particular needs of their population.

Laurier's nationalist critics advocated a very contradictory policy. For them, the federal government should intervene to protect the francophone minorities, going over the heads of the provincial governments if necessary. On the other hand, there was no question of Ottawa's intervening in any way in the affairs of the Quebec government. In other words, for the nationalists, only the autonomy of the province of Quebec mattered. Laurier's position was more consistent: the federal government should *encourage* the English provinces to respect the rights of the francophone minority, but it had to avoid using the special powers granted to it by the constitution to *force* them to do so. If it were to intervene directly in the field of education, an exclusive provincial jurisdiction, the resulting crisis would be more harmful to the minority than any other policy would. In addition, the precedent this would create could one day be turned against the province of Quebec.

BILINGUALISM—Although he was not a proponent of "official bilingualism"—very few thought in those terms at the turn of the twentieth century—Laurier was an advocate of individual bilingualism. In particular, he felt that francophones should learn English, since anyone who did not know the language of the majority would inevitably have limited prospects: "No man on this continent is equipped for the battle of life unless he has an English education." In his correspondence with Émilie Lavergne, he strongly suggested she make sure her son, Armand, learned English: "He does not know that at 20, could he speak and write English as currently and fluently as French, his start in the world would be immeasurably advanced." Armand was opposed to the idea, which led Laurier to say that "they have, at college, put the most absurd ideas in his head [which] may prevent him from acquiring that language."

"SUNNY WAYS"—Since education was clearly the responsibility of the provincial governments, federal members of Parliament found themselves in a sensitive position in each of those controversies. This was particularly the case with the Liberals, given their fierce defence of provincial autonomy. The British North America Act gave Ottawa certain tools for protecting the rights of minorities, such as the power to disallow a provincial law. The 1870 law creating the province of Manitoba even provided the federal government with the specific power to intervene if the rights of the local Catholics or Protestants were violated by a provincial law. It was this power that, under pressure from its Quebec MPs, the then Conservative government promised to use when controversy broke out over the Manitoba Schools Question in 1890. However, it seems that the Tories were not in much of a hurry to make good on this promise. Twice they referred the matter to the courts in the hope that they would decide for them which course to follow. (Proof that politicians did not wait for the adoption of the Canadian Charter of Rights and Freedoms to pass their hot potatoes to judges!)

When, after several years of legal wrangling, the Privy Council in London authorized federal intervention, Ottawa issued a "remedial order" instructing Manitoba to re-establish Catholics' rights. The provincial government refused to comply. The Conservatives then introduced "remedial legislation" that would force the reopening of Catholic schools in the province. The affair resulted in a crisis within the Mackenzie Bowell government (1894–1896) and the resignation of seven ministers.

Although the Conservative government's coercive approach won the enthusiastic approval of the clergy, Laurier, then Opposition leader, denounced it. He proposed another course of action, one that would reconcile the defence of the education rights of minorities with respect for provincial autonomy. This course was typical of the famous "sunny ways," the approach that best sums up his political and personal philosophy. He took the expression from Aesop's fable "The North Wind and the Sun":

> The North Wind and the Sun were disputing which was the stronger when a traveller came along wrapped in a warm cloak. They agreed that the one who first succeeded in making the traveller take his cloak off should be considered the stronger of the two. The North Wind blew as hard as he could, but the more he blew, the more closely the traveller folded his cloak around him; and at last the North Wind gave up the attempt. Then the Sun shone out warmly, and immediately the traveller took off his cloak. And so the North Wind was obliged to confess that the Sun was the stronger of the two.

Laurier provided the following explanation during a tour of Ontario when the Manitoba schools crisis was at its worst: "Well, sir, the government are very windy. They have blown and raged and threatened and the more they have raged and blown, the more that man Greenway [the premier of Manitoba] has stuck to his coat. If it were in my power, I would try the sunny way. I would approach this man Greenway with the sunny way of patriotism, asking him to be just and to be fair, asking him to be generous to the minority, in order that we may have peace among all the creeds and races which it has pleased God to bring upon this corner of our common country."

Was Laurier naïve? He was certainly quite idealistic regarding the power of reason and good faith. He sincerely believed that appealing to reflection and fair play was sufficient to persuade men to adopt just policies. Furthermore, the "sunny ways" were not always as unrealistic as they might appear. To Laurier, there was simply no other way for the federal government to get the provincial governments to respect the rights of minorities. He knew that if he supported the approach of the Conservative government, he would face a crisis within his own party. He also knew that, when all was said and done, the federal government's ability to make the province obey remedial legislation was non-existent. If

Manitoba refused to comply, what could Ottawa do? Create its own school system? Send inspectors to monitor what was happening in the province's schools? Send in the Mounties?

Laurier's pragmatism was also the reason he avoided taking a clear position on this issue as long as he was in Opposition. What solution did he propose? Negotiations with the provincial government. But what else? An investigation to determine what was really happening in the schools of Manitoba. This allowed him to denounce any abuses *possibly* being committed, while refusing to state that there actually was abuse: "*If it is true* that under the guise of public schools, Protestant schools are being continued, and that Roman Catholics are forced, under the law, to attend what are in reality Protestant schools … *If that statement is true*, though my life as a political man should be ended forever, what I say now and shall be prepared to repeat, and would repeat on every platform in Ontario, every platform in Manitoba, nay, every Orange lodge throughout the land, is that the Catholic minority has been subjected to a most infamous tyranny."

This rhetorical tactic was typical of Laurier: saying a thing without really saying it, the art of satisfying one side without displeasing the other. Thus he could present himself to the francophone Catholics as the defender of their rights while swearing to the anglophone Protestants that he had no intention of intervening in the educational affairs of Manitoba to re-establish the "papist" schools. The historian Réal Bélanger does not feel that this case is an example of "profitable political realism": "It was a very short-sighted political realism, because it could have proven quite costly for the Catholic minority and the principle of cultural duality that was being applied in a large part of Canada." But what was the alternative? If Laurier had supported the idea of remedial legislation, would the rights of the Catholic minority have been better respected by the provincial government? What would have been the reaction of anglophone Canadians to authoritarian intervention by Ottawa? What repercussions would their discontent have had for the situation of French Canadians across the country?

To Laurier's mind, the only possible solution was through an agreement with the provincial government. And this agreement would be obtained only if the Liberals formed the next federal government. Hence, as leader of the Opposition, he had to perform a balancing act until the next elections.

THE MARCH TO VICTORY

In the spring of 1896, Laurier's second election campaign as Liberal leader took place. He again faced fierce opposition from the French Canadian Catholic hierarchy. The bishops had not forgiven him for failing to support the Catholics of Manitoba unconditionally. To attack him, they quoted a courageous speech he had made in the House on March 3 of that year, in which he declared he would not have his policy on schools dictated by the church he belonged to: "So long as I have a seat in this House, so long as I occupy the position I do now, whenever it shall become my duty to take a stand upon any question whatever, that stand I will take not upon grounds of Roman Catholicism, not upon grounds of Protestantism, but upon grounds which can appeal to the conscience of all men, irrespective of their particular faith, upon grounds which can be occupied by all men who love justice, freedom and toleration."

"The man who speaks thus," said the old bishop of Trois-Rivières, Msgr. Louis-François Laflèche, "formulates a doctrine entirely opposed to the Catholic doctrine, that is to say, that a Catholic is not bound to be a Catholic in his public life. Under the circumstances, a Catholic cannot under pain of sinning in a grave matter vote for the chief of a party who has formulated so publicly such an error." The church ordered all parish priests to read from the pulpit a pastoral letter reminding the faithful that the hierarchy supported the Conservatives' approach on the Manitoba Schools Question.

Touring Quebec, the archbishop of Saint-Boniface, Msgr. Adélard Langevin, "beseeched" Catholics "to elect only members of Parliament who will respect the right to justice, and who are prepared to give the minority in Manitoba its rights in education. I have no intention of becoming involved in politics, but this is a religious matter that falls under my jurisdiction, and on which you must heed my advice."

Although the bishops campaigned against Laurier, other factors played in favour of the Liberals. The Conservative government, which had been in power for eighteen years, was showing its age. The great Macdonald had died two months after the 1891 election. Having watched the Old Leader's masterful management of his troops since his own arrival in Ottawa, Laurier said: "The fact that during all these years he maintained unimpaired, not only the confidence, but the devotion—the ardent devotion—the affection of his party, is evidence that, besides these higher qualities of statesmanship to which we were the daily witnesses, he was also endowed with this inner, subtle, indefinable characteristic of soul that wins and keeps the hearts of man." Some years later, the same would be said of Laurier, although the two men were made of very different stuff. Each in his own way had an intimate knowledge of human nature and was able to use that knowledge to achieve his ends. Political leaders who do not master that science, that art, rarely enjoy long careers.

After Macdonald's death, the Tories had great difficulty finding a healthy and effective successor. John Abbott had to resign in 1892 for health reasons; John Thompson passed away in 1894; Mackenzie Bowell had to step down after the mutiny that followed the tabling of the remedial bill. It was thus the energetic and experienced Charles Tupper, sixty-four years old, who led the Conservative troops in the 1896 campaign. But the government was so worn out and the party so divided on the Manitoba Schools Question that Tupper, in spite of his strengths, was not able to prevent the Tory cabinet from being brought down.

On June 23, 1896, the Liberals won a decisive victory: 117 seats versus 86 for the Conservatives. Quebecers were not as docile in the voting booth as they were in the confessional: 54 percent of the votes and 49 of the 65 seats in the province went to Laurier. Despite the presence of anti-francophone and anti-Catholic feeling, the Liberals obtained substantial support in the English-speaking provinces (41 percent in Ontario, the base of the Orangemen's support).

Wilfrid Laurier was sworn in as prime minister of the Dominion of Canada on July 11, 1896. A French Canadian at the head of the Confederation! If Laurier became a hero—practically a god—in his province, it was first and foremost because he succeeded in doing something very few French Canadians had thought possible. This triumph reflected on all of them; who would now dare consider them second-class citizens?

The new prime minister went right to work. He formed an exceptionally strong Cabinet, drawing members from the ranks of the provincial governments. Premier of Ontario and father of Confederation Oliver Mowat became minister of justice; premier of Nova Scotia William Fielding was given finance; premier of New Brunswick Andrew Blair was given railways. The outstanding organizer Israël Tarte was also appointed to the Cabinet.

The first task of the new Cabinet was, of course, to solve the problem of the Manitoba schools. It would take four months of negotiations between the federal and provincial governments to achieve that. Did the Laurier government abandon the Catholic minority, as historian Bélanger feels it did? Certainly, there would no longer be separate schools, contrary to the provisions of the Manitoba Act of 1870. The province would have a single education system controlled by the provincial government. The curriculum and textbooks would be chosen by the province's department of education, not by the priests. And in many schools, francophone Catholics would be in the minority, which would increase the risk of assimilation.

This being said, where parents requested it, students could take religion classes at the end of the day, from 3:30 to 4 P.M. In any school with a significant number of Catholic students, the school board would have to hire Catholic teachers for them. Finally, francophone children could take some of their classes in French in so-called bilingual schools. It was certainly a long way from the separate schools that had existed until then; but neither would the schools be neutral and unilingual, as the McCarthys of the country had wished.

The Catholic Church led a fierce campaign against this compromise, even going so far as to put the Quebec City newspaper *L'Électeur* on the Index because it defended the Liberal position. Did the bishops really have the best interests of the students at heart or were they only fighting to maintain their control over education? *La Semaine Religieuse*, the organ of the Montreal archdiocese, commented: "The system of elementary schools they want to impose on the children of our brothers in Manitoba will fatally dry up in the souls of the young generations the sap of the virtues, strengths and noble aspirations that embody

Catholic and French nations. It is not with a half hour of catechism and a few meagre French lessons that this harm will be remedied."

It should be pointed out here that in most of these controversies, it was the religious aspect of the problem that was at the centre of debate, more than the language question. In the negotiations between the Laurier and Greenway governments, the parties quite quickly agreed that teaching could be done in both languages in schools where there were at least ten children whose mother tongue was French. On the place of religion in the schools, however, the discussion was contentious. And in the final agreement, the language question is dispatched in five lines, with all the rest of the document detailing the terms and conditions with regard to religious education.

A GREAT GESTURE

In 1905, nine years after Laurier took power as prime minister, the time came for the creation of two new provinces in the West. The controversy over schools began again. The North-West Territories Act (1875) protected the Catholic minority's right to separate schools. Already, however, the territorial government had limited this right, putting separate schools under its control through two ordinances that made the system in the Territories similar to the one provided for Manitoba under the Laurier–Greenway agreement.

When he introduced the bills creating Saskatchewan and Alberta (the Autonomy Bills, 1905), Laurier seemed, quite uncharacteristically, ready to go on the offensive. Without even notifying the powerful Clifford Sifton, who represented the West in the Cabinet, he proposed to the House that section 93 of the British North America Act be applied to the new provinces—in other words, that the Catholic minority be guaranteed a separate school system. There was cheering in Quebec and outrage in the English provinces. The Orangemen began to agitate, Sifton resigned, and Fielding, the minister of finance, threatened to do the same. Many Liberals were worried. What about provincial autonomy? What about the "sunny ways"?

Laurier was so upset by the reaction that he quickly backed down. To calm the storm, he claimed there had been a misunderstanding, that he had never intended to do anything other than protect the status quo. That version of things, however, is not very plausible. An analysis of his correspondence by the historian Réal Bélanger is quite convincing in this regard. For example, Laurier wrote to Manitoba Liberal John Donald Cameron: "I would not impose separate schools today upon the Territories, if they had not been herein introduced in 1875, with the avowed statement that they were to be part of the system of separate schools as organized at the time of Confederation." His intention to impose a return to separate schools was therefore clear. Otherwise, why would he have made a point of keeping Sifton at a distance?

According to Bélanger, Laurier wanted to attempt "a great gesture," "to go back to the spirit of the Fathers of Confederation, to return to the compromise written into the Constitution of 1867, and finally to fulfill the wishes of the minority and, beyond that, those of Quebec itself." Another biographer, Joseph Schull, also speaks of a "great gesture, the turning back to the spirit of Confederation," which would bring the Liberals big gains in Quebec. The journalist John Wesley Dafoe, who knew Laurier very well, thought the prime minister "knew precisely what he was doing" and had chosen, knowingly, to place his colleagues before "an accomplished fact, leaving no alternative to submission but a palace rebellion which he felt confident no one would attempt." His official biographer, Oscar Skelton, attributes Laurier's attempt to frustration: "There was undoubtedly in his present stand a more lively sympathy with the minority's position than in 1896, born of growing conservatism, or of the irritation at Ontario's insistence ... that Québec must provide all the sacrifices on the altar of harmony."

Whether it was an error in judgment or rashness, it was uncharacteristic of the man. Laurier was perfectly aware, when he was drafting the laws, that the matter was explosive. He must have known that if he tried to go too far, he would divide not only the public but his own party. Was he going to take that risk for a scattered minority that represented barely 5 percent of the population of the Territories? Nor was it his way of doing things to introduce a bill on such an important subject without completely understanding its meaning. Perhaps, having won his third election victory a few months earlier, he felt he could impose his views on his party. One thing is certain—he was stunned by the reaction, and especially by Sifton's resignation. The Autonomy Bills were amended: francophone Catholics in the two new provinces would be able to take religion classes after school hours and study French in elementary school, in separate buildings. However, these schools would be administered by the provincial government, which would have full authority over the curriculum.

Henri Bourassa, who was still a member of the Liberal caucus, led the charge along with some of the clergy. "This amendment is not in keeping with the Constitution, is not in keeping with our rights, is not sufficient, is not acceptable. With this amendment, the teaching of French and religion would be illusory," he declared in front of a crowd gathered in the Monument National theatre in Montreal. He argued that if the Liberal members of Parliament from Quebec stood their ground, they could persuade their colleagues from the other provinces to support the original version of the Autonomy Bills. He was not as astute a politician as his leader. Laurier had immediately understood that his party could be torn apart. Sifton and Fielding were his most important ministers, and he could not afford to ignore their dissatisfaction. He wanted to stay in power, obviously. Above all, he knew that a minority is rarely in a position to impose its views and that, if it tried to do so, it risked losing everything. He was able to convince the moderates on both sides, including those among the clergy.

At this time, a revealing conversation took place between Laurier and the young member of Parliament Armand Lavergne, Émilie's son, who as we saw was a follower of Bourassa:

> Lavergne: All we asked for was rights, all rights, for Catholics.
> Laurier: Certainly, my dear Armand. But anyone who wants all his rights is obliged to fight almost

constantly. Is it wise to fight ... especially when
you are not the strongest one?
Lavergne: Honour ...
Laurier: Peace ...

Peace. Laurier did not want it only for partisan reasons. He was profoundly convinced that the Catholic minority could not come out the winner in a conflict. To fight for honour is certainly heroic. But when you are the weaker one, it results in death.

In hindsight, we must conclude that the concessions Laurier obtained from the provincial governments in the West were far from sufficient to ensure the survival of French in that vast region. It would take Trudeau's Official Languages Act and Charter of Rights and Freedoms, and the ensuing judgments of the Supreme Court, to prevent the complete assimilation of francophones outside Quebec. However, in 1896 and 1905, Laurier would not have been able to get such measures accepted by an anglophone population that was steeped in imperialist propaganda, that hated everything remotely associated with the pope, and that was worried that the influx of immigrants would threaten the English character of Canada. Nor would the prime minister have been able to impose them, contrary to what the clergy and the nationalists naïvely believed. Had he tried, his party would have splintered and he would have lost power.

Laurier therefore did his best to convince the majority that certain privileges had to be granted to the Catholic minority. "Catholics in this country are in the minority. With tact and firmness, they can still command respect," he wrote in 1898 to one of his envoys to Rome, Abbé Proulx. In the short term, he was proven right. However, in the following years, provincial governments moved quickly to adopt measures limiting the impact of the concessions that had been made.

Laurier's hedging caused him to lose some prestige in Quebec. Then as now, people there love those who fight to the finish, who prefer honour to power; those who govern and therefore have to be concerned with preserving peace usually come in for heavy criticism. Some historians think the linguistic battles of that period brought about the birth of modern nationalism in Quebec. One thing is certain, Laurier could sense that he was losing the hearts of Quebecers: "Our friend, Bourassa, has begun in Québec a campaign that may well cause us trouble," he wrote to a Liberal senator.

However, Laurier's point of view was implacably logical: a minority has to fight to defend its rights, but it has to accept compromises, or else it will inevitably be the loser.

Yet, at the same time, the majority has to show openness and generosity, or else it will always have to face the hostility of the minority, and the survival of the shared country will be compromised. Laurier was idealistic in his pragmatism, and he relied on moderation and reason in an area where emotion, prejudice, and rancour dominated on both sides. He himself often bemoaned this situation: "There are questions about which it is impossible to reason with some people."

A TRAGIC DECLINE

A decade later, Laurier witnessed the decline of his vision of the rights of the francophone Catholic minority without being able to do anything about it—even losing the support of his own party. For the man, for the politician, it was nothing less than a tragedy.

Regulation 17, adopted in 1912 by the Ontario government, was aimed not at the Catholic religion, but at the French language. There was no question of abolishing separate schools in the province, since their existence was guaranteed by the British North America Act. It was, however, quite possible, on the pretext of dealing with an education problem—the poor quality of English among francophones—to reduce the teaching of French to a minimal part of the curriculum. Some people clearly expressed the real motive behind this policy—fear of a French Catholic "invasion" of the province (a complete fabrication). Their slogan was simple, and therefore appealing: "One nation, one language."

Regulation 17 prohibited teaching in French after grade one of elementary school. French could be taught as a separate subject, but everything else in the curriculum had to be taught in English. Unlike the situation in the West, the francophones of Ontario were not a small, scattered minority; the policy was an insult to two hundred thousand people who possessed well-established institutions.

Laurier, now seventy, was in the Opposition, following his defeat by Robert Borden's Conservatives in 1911, and he was powerless. However, he could not keep quiet. "If I were to remain silent under such circumstances I would certainly lose my own self-esteem and respect," he wrote to Fielding. In May 1916, he had the future Liberal star from Quebec, Ernest Lapointe, present a motion in which the House of Commons "respectfully suggests to the Legislative Assembly of Ontario the wisdom of making it clear that the privilege of children of French parentage of being taught in their mother tongue be not interfered with."

Tension was already high in the country because of disagreement between French and English Canadians on participation in the First World War. Many anglophones were accusing French Canadians of not enlisting in sufficient numbers in support of such a just cause, and they were demanding conscription. In this context, anglophones were even less inclined than usual to be sympathetic to the francophones' educational demands. And speeches by nationalist leaders comparing English Canadians to the "Boches" hardly calmed them down.

Laurier did not suggest that a solution be imposed on the government of Ontario; he remained faithful to the principle of provincial autonomy. All Lapointe's motion did was "respectfully suggest" to Ontario that it allow francophone children to be educated in French while ensuring that they learned English. "I want every child in the province of Ontario to have an English education," he explained to Parliament. "Wherever he may go on this continent, I want him to be able to speak the language of the great majority of the people of this continent.... When I ask that every child of my own race should receive an English education, will you refuse us the privilege of education also in the language of our mothers and our fathers? That is all I ask today; I ask nothing more than that.... Is that an unnatural demand? Is that an obnoxious demand? Will the concession of it do harm to anybody?"

Despite the quality of the speech, Laurier's logic, his

nobility, there was consternation in the Liberal ranks. With the winds of intolerance sweeping through the ridings of English Canada, voting in favour of such a motion seemed suicidal. It was reported to the leader that the Liberal members of Parliament from Quebec and the Maritimes were in favour of the Lapointe motion, while those from the West and Ontario were against it. Anger overcame Laurier's usual poise; after he had made so many compromises to satisfy the demands of the English speaking, how could his own MPs refuse him such a small thing? He took a sheet of paper, picked up his pen, and wrote: "I am resigning and shall announce my resignation in the House this afternoon." The news travelled like lightning through the Liberal caucus. Panicking, most of the Liberal members immediately rallied behind their leader. Nevertheless, when it came time for the vote, eleven Liberals from the West went against the motion.

Laurier's moral authority over the country, and over the Liberal Party, was further weakened. He had hoped to convince through words, through reason, through an appeal to the ideals of Confederation, but this time he had failed. At the very time when Ontario was implementing Regulation 17, the government of Manitoba was rescinding the section of the Laurier–Greenway agreement that allowed the teaching of French to francophone children. Worried, Laurier reflected: "We have reached a critical period in the development of Confederation, with regard to the rights of the French language. Unfortunately, the BNA Act contains only one article on this subject, and the rights which are conferred upon us are very restricted alike in letter and in spirit.... What are the rights of the French language in the matter of education?"

But in spite of the intolerance shown by the Orangemen and the inability of the anglophone moderates to resist them as he did the radical nationalists and the clergy, the old man remained convinced that his approach was the only valid one: "In constitutional countries it is by persuasion, by moderation that in the end right triumphs." Still, he apperently became convinced that a member of the minority could not persuade the anglophones to make the compromises needed: "It was a mistake for a French Roman Catholic to take the leadership. I told Blake thirty years ago," he wrote. A mistake? Did Laurier really believe what he was saying? If so, that did not prevent him from remaining in his position in spite of his advanced age.

CHAPTER 3

The Duel

It is impossible to satisfy Mr. Bourassa.
WILFRID LAURIER, 1917

When he comes to the gates of paradise, the first thing
Mr. Laurier will do will be to suggest an honourable
compromise between God and Satan.
HENRI BOURASSA, 1910

During the Imperial Conference of 1911, Laurier made
friends with his counterpart from South Africa, Louis Botha.
Conciliators by nature and admirers of British values and
institutions, Laurier and Botha both faced powerful nationalist movements among their compatriots, the French
Canadians for Laurier, and the Boers for Botha. The two
men corresponded regularly in the years that followed. In
1916, Botha asked his friend about the situation in Canada:
"It is difficult to follow political issues in Canada, as the
information we obtain is so meagre. Still, there is one matter
which has been receiving attention here and that is in
connection with one Borassa [*sic*]. I am unable to follow his
attitude altogether, because I know too little about it, but

some of my political opponents are quoting him as shewing that their political views are identical with views held by a large section in other Dominions. Has he really a large following, and is he the mouthpiece of a large section of the Canadian people?"

The fact that the prime minister of South Africa had heard of Henri Bourassa's activities shows the extraordinary impact of the nationalist leader not only on French Canadians but also on other nationalist movements in the Empire. It is clear that of all the political struggles Laurier fought, the one against Bourassa was the hardest and the most painful.

Laurier had become prime minister in large part thanks to support from the province of Quebec. As I stated above, the man was practically worshipped by his French Canadian compatriots. With the years, however, francophones' loyalty to him dwindled, undermined by the attacks of Bourassa, who was a brilliant intellectual and orator. Laurier began to fear that his province would slip from his grasp. Not only would he be out of power but his very definition of Canada would be threatened. According to the journalist John W. Dafoe, his contemporary, he came to fear Bourassa "with a fear that in the end became an obsession." To Botha, who wanted to know more about this "Borassa," Laurier replied:

"Bourassa is a man of great ability, but his ability is negative and destructive. He will never accomplish anything constructive or of benefit to any cause which he may espouse."

The duel between the two men was painful not only because it was between French Canadians but also because they knew each other so well. Laurier had brought Bourassa into the House of Commons by recruiting him as the Liberal candidate in Labelle, in the Outaouais region, in the 1896 election. Bourassa was then twenty-eight years old, and Laurier was fifty-five. Having inherited the largest portion of the Montebello estate of his illustrious ancestor Louis-Joseph Papineau, the young man was free of financial cares and was trying his hand at politics and journalism. He was attracted by Laurier's eloquence and high ideals. Laurier quickly understood that he was dealing with an exceptional individual: before accepting the Liberal nomination, Bourassa demanded the right to vote against the party if he disagreed with it, and in order to guarantee his independence, he refused to let the Liberal Party fund his campaign.

When he became prime minister, Laurier had high ambitions for his protégé. He immediately gave him a role in the negotiations on the Manitoba schools, and Bourassa faithfully defended the government's position. That would be his last compromise. The two men parted ways soon after.

In the years that followed, Henri Bourassa became the hero and inspiration of the Quebec nationalists. However, his nationalism was closer to Laurier's than to that of the independence movement that later emerged from the current of thought he led. In fact, Bourassa was opposed to "separatism" and the confinement of French Canadians to the province of Quebec. He dreamed of a Canada that was as autonomous as possible within the Empire, a Canada where the two main "races" would have equal status: "We have the right to be of the French language; we have the right to be of the Catholic faith; we have the right to be free under the constitution; we are Canadians above all else; we have as much right to be British as anyone. And we have the right to enjoy these rights throughout Confederation," he declared in Montreal in 1912.

Let us recall Laurier's words at the Saint-Jean-Baptiste festivities in 1889: "We are French-Canadians, but our country is not confined to the territory overshadowed by the Citadelle of Québec; our country is Canada…. What I claim for ourselves is an equal place in the sun, an equal share of justice, of liberty; that share we have; and what we claim for ourselves we are anxious to grant to others."

These two French Canadian leaders both dreamed of a united Canada where the two founding "races" would have equal rights and would be united while maintaining their differences. These similarities led André Laurendeau, an illustrious successor of Bourassa as editor of the newspaper *Le Devoir*, to wonder "if Bourassa was not influenced much more by Laurier than has been recognized."

This being said, there was a huge difference between the two men's approaches toward achieving their ideal. For Laurier, the only way for francophones to have their "equal place in the sun" was to negotiate with their anglophone partners, which meant that each side would have to make compromises; no other course was possible for a minority. Bourassa, on the other hand, felt that they had to win respect by refusing to back down on their principles. Steadiness in defending their rights, he felt, would compensate for their small numbers.

Their approaches differed because the two men's personalities were diametrically opposed. Bourassa was rational, uncompromising, moralistic, and a practising Catholic. To him, all compromise was dishonourable. His political career, which was marked by sudden changes, circumstantial alliances, and resignations, illustrates this refusal to make any accommodation. To him, the rights of francophone Catholics were sacred, whatever their number, whatever their distribution in a given region. Imperialism was harmful and no concession should be made to it, whatever the wishes of the majority of the Canadian population. We find the best example of this attitude in his refusal to accept the deployment of a volunteer regiment (not conscripts, volunteers!) to South Africa during the Boer War (1899–1902). "To govern is to have the courage, at a given moment, to risk power to save a principle!" he told his leader at that time. Laurier sighed: "Ah, my dear young friend, you have not a practical mind."

Bourassa recounted another revealing conversation, one that occurred a few years later when Laurier was getting ready to table the Autonomy Bills. Bourassa was worried that Sifton had not been informed of the content of the bills. Laurier answered him: "We did not go into those details. My dear Henri, you have such a French mind! I, however, float in the ambient air." Bourassa defended principles against all opposition, often against all realism. Laurier also defended principles, but his first principles were the unity of the country and of the Liberal Party.

WHEN BOURASSA WAS RIGHT

Generally speaking, it is only through pragmatism that a country as complex as Canada can be governed; this was as true in Laurier's day as it is today. However, there were times when Laurier's "practical solution" was frankly pathetic, rare occasions when he was not able to put a cloak of heroism on his pragmatism. This happened during a brief debate in the House of Commons on a motion presented by Bourassa's companion in arms, Armand Lavergne, proposing that "the French language, which in virtue of the constitution is official, be placed on a footing of equality with the English language in all public matters—for instance, in the coinage of moneys and in the administration of postal affairs." This was in 1907—six decades before Trudeau, Lavergne and Bourassa were proposing official bilingualism. In the course of this debate, Bourassa described the situation of French within the federal administration: "Go into some of the departments of this government; and apart from some of the messengers, you will find nobody, from the head to the lowest, who understands a word of French.... In most of the departments, when letters are received in French, they are replied to in English. If you write a letter in French for the convenience of some French constituent of yours, you will be replied in English, and sometimes the English will be written by a French speaking official."

To Bourassa, the solution was simple: "In every department of this federal government there should be a sufficient number of officials capable of speaking both languages so as to give full satisfaction to both races.... I claim it may tend to the harmony of the French-speaking and the English-speaking races if that constitutional fact, that very practical fact, is given effect to in small matters as well as the great."

The English-speaking members of Parliament were far from favourable. To some, it was a trivial matter. To others, such as the Orange leader T.S. Sproule, "in Canada we are in an English-speaking country.... I disagree with the contention of the hon. Gentleman that the two languages should be on an equal footing.... We will suppose, for instance, that the French gradually become fewer and fewer in Canada until there are not 10,000, or not one hundred of them in Canada; would it be a common sense thing to say that you should keep up everything in the French language just as you do today? I do not think so."

What did Laurier say? He proposed an amendment to Lavergne's motion, stating that "the French language is, in fact as well as by the constitution, on a footing of equality with the English language"—which was patently false. He used a tortuous argument to support this statement, giving as evidence of the equality of the two languages the fact that Lavergne had chosen to defend his motion in English. He cited the example of Louis-Hippolyte LaFontaine, who had made his first speech to the Parliament of United Canada in

French, in 1842, when that language had no official status: "Having obtained that right however, he did not choose to go any further. He spoke most of the time in English.... Instead of affirming pedantically on every occasion our right to speak the French language, it is sufficient for me, it is sufficient for all French Canadians, I am sure, that we have obtained the right to speak French and to use our mother tongue on the floor of this parliament.... It is not necessary to use French where everyone understands English, but obviously the French should be used when it is more convenient for the people."

To Laurier, in other words, the right to use the French language existed in theory and that was sufficient, at least for francophones who could get along in English. If this view had not been gradually abandoned by federal politicians, it would have led inevitably to the assimilation of francophones outside Quebec, and to a revolt of those within Quebec. This time, it was Bourassa who was right: for French to survive in Canada, francophones had to insist on the equality of the two founding languages in national institutions. They had to be able to address the federal government and be replied to in their own language. Only in this way would they come to consider the government of Canada *their* government.

Unwavering on all matters, Bourassa would bow only to

one master, the church. At a private audience with Pope Pius XI in 1926, he was reprimanded as follows: "The main obstacle to the action of the Papacy and the Church in the world … is the substitution of nationalism for Catholicism." Shaken, Bourassa devoted the rest of his life to a crusade against "immoderate nationalism." He took to concluding his speeches by asking his listeners to say a prayer. In front of the pope, the oak tree had suddenly become a reed. In contrast, Laurier fought with all his strength when the bishops tried to impose their political views on the country. And the reed became an oak tree!

OPEN WAR

The break between the two men came in 1899 during the debate on Canada's participation in the Boer War. From that time on, Bourassa's speeches attacked his former mentor with increasing violence. Although Laurier was not easily irritated, he was upset by the words of the man for whom he had such great expectations. In 1907, he wrote to a Liberal Party activist: "Bourassa has a major flaw: he has no sense of proportion.… He fights his friends as violently as he fights his enemies; he becomes drunk on his own words; he gets annoyed when he is contradicted; he ends up overshooting his mark; and he lets himself unconsciously slip from friendly criticism to open war." In a speech at the Monument National theatre in Montreal in the fall of 1910, he added: "[Bourassa] has come to have a disagreeable need to slander, disparage and debase his country to prevent it from fulfilling the obligations national dignity demands of it."

Bourassa's attacks had an impact. Laurier continued to win the majority of seats in the province, but his influence was waning. We see evidence of this in November 1910, when Bourassa's candidate won a by-election in Drummond-Arthabaska, which was formerly Laurier's own riding and where he still had a house. On the day of the vote, Bourassa fired a new salvo toward him: "The glory of the Great Man is declining, and it is turning to shit." It was vulgar, but an accurate prediction: the following year, Laurier's government was defeated by Robert Borden's Conservatives. The Tories had made a tactical agreement with Bourassa so that in the province of Quebec, they would not run against "autonomist candidates" who had his blessing. Although the Conservatives were more imperialistic than the Liberals, for a short time they shared an objective with the nationalists: to beat Laurier. "I admire Mr. Laurier as a private man," declared Bourassa at a huge opposition rally in Saint-Hyacinthe. "But the most charming private men and the most eloquent public men do not deserve that we sacrifice the rights and freedom of a whole people." Laurier, he said, "has deceived us." Bourassa, who had founded the newspaper *Le Devoir* the year before, hoped that the presence of a nationalist bloc in the House of Commons would prevent the federal government from yielding to the sirens of imperialism. The result was that the autonomist–conservative alliance won twenty-seven seats in the province of Quebec, sixteen more than the Conservatives alone had in the previous election. However, the new prime minister, Robert Borden, had a comfortable majority; contrary to what Bourassa had envisioned, the Tory leader did not need the support of the nationalists to govern.

RECONCILIATION

Six years later, there was an unexpected rapprochement between the former prime minister and the journalist— unexpected because only a year before, Bourassa had called Laurier "the most nefarious man in the whole of Canada." However, circumstances had changed. The First World War was dragging on and the allied troops were being decimated. Borden felt he had no choice but to introduce conscription. The elderly Laurier was opposed, and it was that opposition that made reconciliation with Bourassa possible.

Bourassa may also have felt sympathy for the man who

had been abandoned by many Liberals on this issue. No doubt he saw the troubles of his former leader as a confirmation of his own views. At any rate, he liked to recount that during a meeting they had had in Ottawa in the summer of 1917, Laurier "pressed me to his heart and said, 'Bourassa, you predicted eleven years ago what is happening to me today. I know now who my real friends are.'" Was Laurier acknowledging that Bourassa had been right, that he should have joined ranks with the French Canadian nationalists—his "real friends"—rather than making a deal with the English Canadians? Was he, as the historian Réal Bélanger feels, assessing "the failure of his political career"? Do not for one minute believe this. Although we should not minimize the tragedy that the events of 1917 represented for Laurier, it is clear that he lost neither hope nor conviction. In a letter to the young lawyer Léon-Mercier Gouin in July 1918, he reiterated his faith in the approach he had always taken: "We mustn't forget, as you remind me with so much truth, that the Canadian Confederation was a compromise. Nor must we forget that it is almost always in compromise that we find the solutions to the thorniest problems."

The fact remains that during the election campaign of 1917, Bourassa gave his support to the Liberals because they were against the introduction of conscription. If one of the two duelling partners had to acknowledge the failure of his strategy, it was Bourassa. The alliance he had formed with the Conservatives had backfired against French Canadians just as Laurier had predicted.

During the summer of 1918, an old and ill Laurier was trying to regain his strength at the home of his friend Laurent-Olivier David in the Laurentians when Bourassa came to visit him. Zoé was suspicious; she had not forgiven him. Sir Wilfrid, however, was in a very good mood. He questioned his guest about everything, encouraging him to talk, and Bourassa liked nothing better than holding forth. Here is how Bourassa recounted what followed: "And I talked and talked. At one point, Mr. Laurier gave his wife an amused glance and she turned to me attentively. 'So, Zoé, didn't I tell you he could be charming?' And I realized then what was happening. My old friend was trying to create a sympathetic atmosphere around me. That was pure Laurier."

Many years after Laurier's death, in a speech in the House of Commons, Bourassa shared his feelings about the former prime minister: "Laurier knows now that, although I fought against him because of our disagreement on principles, I loved him all my life." And he spoke of "my profound regret for the many bitter words I have spoken in my life, my profound and sincere remorse for the violence of my language."

CHAPTER 4

God and His Men

> I was educated by priests, and amongst young men who
> have become priests. I flatter myself to have sincere friends
> amongst them, and to them at least I can and I do say:
> "Can you find under the sun a happier country, where the
> Catholic church is freer and enjoys greater privileges?"
> WILFRID LAURIER, 1877

Since its construction in 1852, the Quebec Music Hall had
been considered one of the most beautiful venues in North
America. Located not far from where the Château Frontenac
Hotel stands today, the Music Hall hosted the great music
and theatre performances of the day. On the evening of
June 26, 1877, however, the two thousand people crowded
into the hall were not there to listen to Bach or to enjoy the
humour of Molière. The evening was reserved for politics.
The guest speaker was the rising star of the Liberal Party of
Canada, a certain Wilfrid Laurier. Thirty-five years of age,
he had been sitting in the House of Commons for barely
three years.

Expectations were high, inordinately so. The young
politician had been asked to speak on the current state of

Canadian liberalism. The partisan audience hoped that this new voice would help counteract the incessant attacks of the clergy against the school of thought they belonged to. They would get their wish. "Mr. Laurier opened up a new era in our politics," wrote the Liberal lawyer Charles Langelier in his *Souvenirs politiques.* "In one breath, with one master stroke, he dissipated all the old prejudices, vanquished the hydra of fanaticism and showed the true colours of the Liberal Party." This judgment was obviously overenthusiastic; nevertheless, the press coverage from the period shows that it was indeed a decisive event, for Laurier as well as the Liberal Party.

To better appreciate it, we have to look back briefly at the context of the period. In the province of Quebec, Conservative politicians were generally more favourable than Liberals to intervention by the church in public affairs. The radicals among them, the Castors,* defended ultramontanist ideas; they included many powerful bishops, such as Msgr. Ignace Bourget of Montreal and Msgr. Louis-François Laflèche of Trois-Rivières. The Liberals were more reserved regarding the role of the clergy outside the church. The Liberal Party also had its radicals, the Rouges, who were

---

* Their name comes from the pseudonym chosen by one of them to sign a pamphlet.

staunchly anticlerical. Taking their inspiration from the French republicans, they advocated, among other things, education for all under government control.

Far from conceding anything to the state, the ultramontanists wanted to strengthen the clergy's control of the province. For example, the "Catholic Program" published by the *Journal de Trois-Rivières* in 1870, which was written by laymen but known to represent the views of Monsignori Bourget and Laflèche, stated that in political matters as in others (education, culture, morality), voters should follow the directives of the church: "Full and entire adhesion to Roman Catholic doctrines in religion, in politics, and in social economy ought to be the first and principal qualification which the Catholic electors should require from the candidate." In a pastoral letter published in 1875, the Episcopate of Quebec recalled the words of Pope Pius IX: "Catholic Liberalism is the most inveterate and the most dangerous enemy of the divine constitution of the Church."

The clergy's attacks made no distinction between the Rouges and moderate Liberals. In the words of Monsignor Bourget, "no Catholic is allowed to proclaim himself a moderate Liberal." "It was practically high treason to call oneself a Liberal," said Langelier. Here again, he was probably exaggerating somewhat, since a substantial number of Liberals had managed to get elected in federal elections since the beginning of Confederation and in fact, starting in 1874, the election in which Laurier himself was first elected, the majority of Quebec members of the House of Commons had been Liberals.

Nevertheless, during election campaigns, some priests had no qualms about terrorizing their parishioners from the pulpit with descriptions of "the abyss of evils into which the partisans of Catholic liberalism would throw you." They preached that voting Liberal was a mortal sin. Interference by the church reached such a level that the Liberals turned to the courts. In 1876, they obtained the annulment of a by-election in the riding of Charlevoix, which had been won by a Conservative, because priests had used their sermons to denounce the Liberal Party. "Liberalism resembles the serpent which crawls in the terrestrial paradise to procure the fall of the human race," one of them had said in a typical attack. The case went to the Supreme Court, which ruled in favour of the Liberals. "There is there an exerting of undue influence of the worst kind, inasmuch as these threats and these declarations fell from the lips of the priests speaking from the pulpit in the name of religion and were addressed to persons ill-instructed and generally well-disposed to follow the counsels of their curés," concluded Judge Jean-Thomas Taschereau.

What did Laurier think of all this? We have seen that as a young lawyer and journalist, he was a Rouge. When he began practising law in Montreal, he was a member of the Institut Canadien, their main meeting place. His articles in *Le Défricheur* were critical of church authority: "Subjects who refuse obedience to authority when it is just and equitable sin against the doctrine of the Church. Similarly, authority that demands obedience when it is arbitrary, unjust or iniquitous—tyrannical, finally—also sins against the doctrine of the Church. And authority that sins in this way against the doctrine of the Church is not entitled to the subject's obedience, and the subject has the right to refuse it." Such opinions earned him the hostility of newspapers that were close to the local clergy. They tried to intimidate the impudent young man by using the harshest terms; in French Canada of the nineteenth century, to be called impious was not without consequences.

Laurier's biographers trace his hostility toward clerical abuse of authority to the seven years he spent at Collège de L'Assomption. Like all the classical colleges of the time, it imposed iron discipline and provided an education imbued with Catholic orthodoxy. Laurier himself described the education provided by these institutions in a letter to Edward Blake in 1882: "The colleges with us are a hot bed of conservatism, and this is how it acts. The education which we receive in all our colleges is in the hands of the priests. Very good men they are indeed, but prejudiced, biased and except upon those branches of knowledge of which they have made a specialty, very ignorant. Very ignorant, especially are they of modern history. The books they have read, all the sources of information to which they have access, are the continental ultramontane books and press. They have there imbibed a horror of the very name liberalism, which permeates the whole of their teaching. Their pupils, when they leave the school, are ignorant but fanatic conservatives." (Despite this unflattering opinion, a few months later, on the fiftieth anniversary of the Collège de L'Assomption, Laurier gave a stirring speech praising his former teachers. And he returned to his alma mater on other occasions, including a moving final visit a few months before his death.)

From adolescence, Laurier distanced himself not only from the church but from the Catholic faith, at least as it was imposed on French Canadians of the time. In his hagiography of Laurier, Laurent-Olivier David said of his friend's youth, "The mysteries and problems of religion tormented his reason." Laurier's scepticism with regard to religion lasted much longer than David suggested. Writing to Émilie Lavergne in March 1892 (he was then fifty), he said: "You have the faith: you can pray. I do wish that I also, I could believe & pray. I most fervently believe in the justice of Him from whom we proceed & to whom we owe all. I believe in the justice & mercy of his laws, eternal like himself; further my faith goes not & I regret it.... Having neither the faith, nor the hope, I try to grow indifferent & to become callous at the blows which all my efforts have not succeeded in averting." We thus see that Laurier believed in the existence of a Supreme Being, but not in the virtues of religious practice.

According to the journalist John Willison, who knew him well, it was around the turn of the century that Laurier returned to the Catholic fold, and "henceforth he was among its faithful communicants." This corresponds to the date of an exchange of letters the Liberal leader had with Monsignor Bourget's successor at the Archdiocese of Montreal, Msgr. Paul Bruchési, who became his friend. In a letter dated April 6, 1899, the archbishop implored him to return to the practice of his religion. Saying that a certain Mr. Geoffrion* had confessed and taken communion at Easter, no doubt for

* Perhaps the radical Liberal Christophe-Alphonse Geoffrion, a member of Laurier's Cabinet, who would die three months later.

the first time in many years, the archbishop asked Laurier to do the same: "And my dear Mr. Laurier, allow me to ask you in the name of my affection for you, have you done so? You must be absolutely with us. And you want this as well, so why wait?" Three days later, the prime minister replied: "I am happy to tell you that your call has been heard and your prayer was granted this very day." Laurier was then almost sixty. Exactly what induced him to grant the archbishop's wishes? He does not say clearly: "If I were close to Your Excellency, you would perhaps agree to hear many things that I would have to say about the state of my soul for many years. Perhaps one day I will broach this subject. Today I simply say to you: *Credo: Deus adjuvet fiduciam.*"*

"THERE ARE OUR MODELS!"

Fundamentally moderate, Laurier quickly distanced himself from the anticlerical faction of the Liberal Party. Moreover, except in the paranoid imagination and propaganda of the ultramontanists, the Rouges had been in decline since Confederation. The time was ripe for the distinction Laurier was to make, in his speech of 1877 in Quebec City, between "Catholic liberalism" and "political liberalism."

* I believe: God helps faith.

That evening in June 1877, in front of hundreds of people in the Quebec Music Hall, the member of Parliament for Drummond-Arthabaska must have been very nervous. He had never made a speech to such a distinguished crowd ("the leading men of the country, from the bench, the bar, all the liberal professions, to business, industry and the trades," related one witness). We do not really know why the Club Canadien called on the relatively inexperienced Laurier to address such a sensitive topic. The event was taking place just when the Vatican delegate, Irish bishop George Conroy, was on mission in the province, with instructions to put a stop to the clergy's excessive involvement in political matters.

Laurier's biographer Réal Bélanger describes him searching in his books and reviewing his broad culture for five days to write this important speech. When he arrived in Quebec City, he was prepared. And he went right to the heart of the matter: "I am under no illusion as to the situation of the Liberal Party in Quebec ... I know that in the eyes of a large number of my fellow-countrymen the Liberal Party is a party composed of men of perverse doctrines and dangerous tendencies, pressing knowingly and deliberately towards revolution."

He gave less a speech than a demonstration. Contrary to

the claims of their adversaries, he explained, the Liberals of Canada had nothing to do with the revolutionaries of the Old World. The excesses of liberalism in Europe were not due to the application of liberal principles, any more than the abuses of conservatism could be explained by its principles: "Both [liberalism and conservatism] are susceptible of great good and of great evil." He distanced himself from the bloody abuses carried out in the name of freedom in Europe, and from the "Catholic liberalism" denounced by the pope: "They are not liberals, they are revolutionaries. With these men, we have nothing in common." He pointed out that English liberalism, in contrast to that of continental Europe, had led to progress toward democracy and freedom, without revolution or violence. "What is grander than the history of the great English Liberal party during the present century?" he asked. "Liberals of the Province of Quebec, there are our models, there are our principles, there is our party!" Why would the French-Canadian Church, loyal to the Crown since the Conquest, attack people who took their inspiration from one of the two great parties sitting in Westminster?

Laurier also dissociated himself from the Rouges in Canada, but diplomatically. He obviously did not want to offend anyone in the liberal movement to which he belonged. "The only excuse for these Liberals was their youth; the oldest of them was not more than 22." And he carefully avoided choosing between Papineau, who was a hero to so many French Canadians (including his father), and LaFontaine, who, like him, was a pragmatist: "Both loved their country ardently and passionately. Both devoted their lives to it. Both by different means had no other end in view than to serve it. Both were disinterested and honest. Let us remain contented and satisfied with these memories and seek not to find out who was right and who was wrong."

Laurier then went on the attack, in a particularly daring way. Not only did he defend the Liberals against accusations of anticlericalism but he accused the ultramontanists of doing harm to religion, of "laboriously endeavouring, and unfortunately too effectively, to drag down religion to the level of a political party.... I have too much respect for the faith in which I was born to use it as the basis of a political organization." Here, then, was a Liberal taking up the favourite weapon of the ultramontanists, the respect due to the faith, and turning it against them!

One might have expected him to urge the church to stop meddling in politics. He took a more subtle position, and once again, an original one. How could liberals forbid anyone to take part in political debate? "Let the priest speak and preach as he thinks best; such is his right, and no Canadian

Liberal will dispute that right." However, like any right, this one was limited by the rights of other people. The clergy could try to convince the faithful, but it had no right to intimidate them. If it did, it was violating the spirit of responsible government, since the citizens would be prevented from freely choosing who would govern them. In the long run, such an attitude on the part of the church would produce the disorder it wanted at all costs to avoid: "If after each election the will expressed is not the real will of the country, once more you do violence to the Constitution, responsible government is no longer anything but an empty name, and, sooner or later, here as elsewhere, the pressure will culminate in explosion, violence and ruin." What an inspired manoeuvre: accusing the Catholic hierarchy of leading the country toward revolution!

The final passages of this memorable speech are rarely quoted. However, they are the most moving. They reminded French Canadians that their survival on this continent was a kind of miracle. A miracle of which they were the authors, of course, but for which they were also indebted to British pragmatism, sense of justice, and liberalism.

Not far from the site of the Music Hall stood (and still stands) an obelisk erected in 1828 in memory of Generals Montcalm and Wolfe. It bears the following inscription:

Mortem virtus communem
Faman historia
*Monumentum posteritas dedit**

Laurier described how he had been struck by this monument: "What Canadian is there who in going through the streets of this old city, and seeing the monument a few feet from this place, erected to the memory of two brave men, who fell on the same fields of battle in fighting for the possession of this country, but feels proud of his country?" The emotion of the audience was mounting.

> When in this last battle, the cannon spread death among the French ranks, when the old heroes, whom victory had so often followed, saw her at last deserting them, when reclining on the sod, feeling their heart's blood flowing and life departing, they saw, as a consequence of defeat, Quebec in the hands of the enemy and their country forever lost; no doubt their last thoughts turned toward their children, toward those whom they

---

* Valour gave them a common death,
  history a common fame,
  posterity a common monument.

left without protection and without defence; doubtless they saw them persecuted, enslaved, humiliated; and then we may imagine their last breath to have been a cry of despair.

But, if on the other hand, heaven had permitted the veil of the future to be raised before their expiring vision, if heaven permitted them, before their eyes closed forever, to penetrate the unknown, if they could have seen their children free and happy, walking proudly in every rank of society; if they could have seen in the ancient cathedral the seat of honor of the French governors occupied by a French Governor; if they could have seen the spires of churches piercing the azure in every valley from the waters of Gaspé to the plains of Red River; if they could have seen this old flag which reminds us of their greatest victory, triumphantly borne in all our public ceremonies; finally, if they could have seen our free institutions, may we not believe that their last breath was softened to a murmur of thanks to heaven, and that they found consolation as they died.

Laurier had conquered the crowd. Many had tears in their eyes. "At last Liberalism had found the interpreter it sorely needed," declared Oscar D. Skelton. "Had Laurier died at 10 P.M. on 26 June 1877, his place in history would have been assured," said biographer Laurier LaPierre. "There is no disputing that on June 26, 1877, Laurier became a national figure," wrote historian Réal Bélanger.

What were the effects of Laurier's speech? He certainly did not "vanquish the hydra of fanaticism," as Charles Langelier said in his *Souvenirs politiques*. On the contrary, ultramontanism was at its height, and it would take decades for the clergy to stop its political interference. The speech thus had less effect on the Conservatives than on the Liberals, who found a brilliant, charismatic, moderate leader. The future of French Canadian liberalism had seemed dark, but now there was a new sense of hope. We read further in Langelier's memoirs: "The timorous consciences of many Liberals were relieved to hear that this party that had been subjected to so much condemnation deserved the respect of all good citizens and could hold its head high." For Laurier was, in his person, his tone, and his ideas, eminently worthy of respect. It would thus be difficult for the clergy to portray him as Lucifer. The speech hit home because it was pure Laurier: balanced, noble, cultivated. His style contrasted sharply with the demagoguery that dominated the time. Bélanger has found the best description: "Laurier was above all a pragmatic politician" but he was also "capable of rising to ideas."

This event was certainly a turning point in Laurier's career. However, its impact was not sufficient to allow him to avoid a humiliating defeat. Three months later, on October 8, 1877, Prime Minister Alexander Mackenzie appointed him minister of inland revenue. During this period, a member of Parliament had to stand in a by-election before taking a Cabinet post. So here was the new minister, fresh from the triumph of his speech on liberalism, asking the voters of Drummond-Arthabaska, among whom he had been living for a decade, to renew their confidence in him. There should have been no doubt about the outcome.

However, to everyone's surprise, it was the Conservative candidate, the merchant Désiré-Olivier Bourbeau, who won. His victory was a narrow one, only twenty-two votes, but it was no less painful. Laurier and his friends attributed the defeat to the corrupt practices of the Conservatives, but as we know, that party had no monopoly on improprieties. At the very least, we must conclude that despite the enthusiasm aroused by his performance in Quebec City, Laurier was not yet unbeatable in French Canada. Furthermore, liberalism continued to instill a great deal of fear in the population.

The by-election defeat would only be an interlude in Laurier's political career. He persuaded the Liberals to give him another chance. "I am the last card of the party in this province. If I am sent down the party is well nigh gone down completely," he wrote without undue modesty to Mackenzie. One month later, after a campaign in which the Liberal Party went all out, he was elected in Quebec East. "I have unfurled the Liberal standard above the ancient citadel of Québec and there I will keep it waving," he declared. He kept his promise, representing that constituency until his death forty-one years later. Quebec East became a legendary riding; over eight decades, it successfully elected three outstanding French Canadians: Laurier, Ernest Lapointe, and Louis St-Laurent.

The 1877 speech did not persuade the priests to step down from the political pulpit. The following autumn, on the instructions of the Vatican delegate, Monsignor Conroy, the bishops of Quebec published a pastoral letter stating that it was forbidden for priests "to teach in the pulpit or elsewhere that it is a sin to vote for such a candidate or such a party; much more are you forbidden to announce that you will refuse the sacraments for this reason. From the pulpit you will never give your personal opinion." Was Conroy influenced by Laurier's words? That is not very likely, although some historians are convinced that he read the speech. He spent many months in Quebec and it would be very surprising if a single speech by a member of Parliament was the determining factor in his conclusions.

Never before had there been so clear a statement on the limits of political action by priests as the message dictated by Conroy. But as the subsequent political history of Quebec shows, it was not sufficient to change the clergy's behaviour.

VATICAN DIPLOMACY

Laurier learned from these events that the most effective strategy for fighting the excesses of the ultramontanists was through the Vatican. Thus, during the Manitoba schools crisis, he used his diplomatic skills to obtain Rome's support for the compromise negotiated with the Greenway government. That support proved decisive. As I recounted above, the Laurier–Greenway agreement on the teaching of religion and French in the schools of Manitoba had angered the French Canadian bishops. The prime minister sent two successive delegations to the Vatican to ask it to send an investigator to Canada. Luck smiled on Laurier: the man who was sent was a young, earnest priest of Spanish origin, born in London, Rafael Merry del Val, who was destined for a brilliant career in the Curia.

Like many before him, del Val was won over by Laurier's personality. He quickly saw the merits of the prime minister's realistic approach and was convinced that the agreement, while far from perfect, was the best possible under the circumstances. This was the position taken in the encyclical promulgated in 1897 by Pope Leo XIII, *Affari Vos*. In it, the Sovereign Pontiff recognized that the cause of the Manitoba Catholics was a just one. Then, following Laurier, he asked them to accept compromise: "Until they succeed in all of their claims, let them not refuse partial satisfaction. This is why, wherever the law or administration, or the good dispositions of the people, offer some means of lessening the evil, and of warding off some of the dangers, it is absolutely expedient and advantageous that they should make use of them, and derive all the benefit possible from them."

This was a triumph for Laurier's strategy over that of the ultramontanists. However, he knew that the Liberals' chances of success in Quebec would always be diminished if the clergy was against him. He therefore cultivated support among those bishops who, without necessarily being more moderate on fundamental principles, at least were more pragmatic than Bourget and Laflèche. He found a valuable ally in the person of Monsignor Bruchési, although he had campaigned against the Greenway–Laurier agreement in Rome. As mentioned earlier, the two men exchanged many letters and developed a genuine friendship that benefited both of them. Laurier was able to curb the enthusiasm of Félix-Gabriel Marchand's provincial government (1897–1900), which wanted to increase government influence on the education system. And Bruchési supported Laurier in the debate on a bill to make Sunday an obligatory day of rest—the Lord's Day Act (1906)—which was opposed by Bourassa's nationalists.

In religion, Laurier was, as in all things, a moderate, pragmatic liberal. "Conservative in my feelings and my affections," as he described himself, he was wary of excesses, including excesses of piety. "History teaches us," he said in the Commons in 1889, "that it is always in the sacred name of religion that the most violent passions of humankind have been aroused and the most horrible crimes committed." Faith was one thing, but what certain men of the church did with it was another. A few years later, speaking to the young members of the Club National in Montreal, he made a distinction between the resentment one might feel as a liberal regarding certain actions of the clergy, and one's personal convictions: "Let me say to you that you should never allow your religious convictions to be affected by the acts of men. Your convictions are immortal. Their foundation is eternal.

Let your convictions be always calm, serene and superior to the inevitable trials of life. Show to the world that Catholicism is compatible with the exercise of liberty in its highest acceptation."

Laurier gradually returned to Catholicism, although we do not really know by what path. Age was no doubt a factor. With the approach of death, his faith grew deeper, as it does for many people. The last speech of his life, delivered in Ottawa on January 14, 1919, concluded with these words worthy of a sermon: "My hope is every day growing brighter and greater, that the time is not distant when we will all hear the message proclaimed by the angels: 'Glory to God in the Highest. Peace on Earth. Goodwill to Men.'"

CHAPTER 5

The Empire

> I do not pretend to be an imperialist. Neither do I pretend
> to be an anti-imperialist. I am a Canadian first, last and all
> the time.
> **WILFRID LAURIER, 1910**

In June 1897, one year after becoming prime minister,
Laurier took part in the first large-scale Imperial Conference
(then still known as a Colonial Conference), which was held
in London during the celebration of Queen Victoria's
Diamond Jubilee. The heads of government from the
colonies were received with great pomp and ceremony, with
banquet after banquet. "I am not sure whether the British
Empire needs a new constitution, but I am certain that every
Jubilee guest will need one," joked Laurier. Zoé said, "We
have seen royalty close up, we have been invited to the best
houses, and everyone is as friendly as could be." Laurier was
knighted—against his will, he said. Still, he did not object to
having the title attached to his name throughout his career;
he was not as indifferent to honours as he claimed.

It was not out of mere friendliness that the English

treated the colonial representatives so well. They wanted to dazzle them so as to get them to agree to increased participation in the Empire's defence and trade, and eventually the creation of an imperial federation dominated by London. In the United Kingdom imperialist sentiments and ambitions were at their height, based on the conviction not only that British democracy and its institutions were a superior form of government but that the English race itself surpassed all others. According to the colonial secretary, Joseph Chamberlain, the English were destined "to be the predominating force in the future history and civilization of the world."

It was not the elegant evenings in London or the working meetings chaired by Chamberlain that were the basis of Laurier's policy with respect to the ambitions of the British, but rather the towns and the countryside, the newspapers and the ballot boxes of Canada. Aside from religious and linguistic issues, no controversy aroused more contradictory passions in the country than the imperial question, and none so sharply divided French Canadians and their English Canadian compatriots. Consequently, all the decisions that Laurier would make in this area would be dictated by a single objective, the obsession of his career: to avoid the breakup of the country.

Convinced that Canada would become increasingly autonomous over the decades, he would not take any bold initiatives to speed things up. But he would firmly resist all the United Kingdom's moves towards greater integration of the Empire. English Canadian imperialists looked very favourably upon London's efforts, but French Canadian nationalists met them with suspicion, even hostility. Laurier quickly understood that the best way to avoid increasing the tensions between francophones and anglophones was not to rush things one way or the other, but to let history slowly take its course. Laurier would thus be the valiant champion—of the status quo. Historians Ramsay Cook and Craig Brown speak of this as an "unheroic policy."

If this is the case, why is Sir Wilfrid considered a pioneer of Canadian nationalism, the first advocate of Canadian independence from the imperialist impulses of London? For two reasons. First, to say no to Chamberlain, who was then the most influential politician of the most powerful country in the world, may not have been heroic, but it took guts— especially because it also meant ignoring pressure from the powerful Canadian imperialist lobby. In rejecting the plans of the mother country, Laurier was already making a strong gesture of autonomy. Second, through his words, through his class, through his steadfastness during his visits to

London, he gave Canadians a new image of themselves and their country. He made them proud, and that pride—shared by francophones and anglophones alike—would make a powerful contribution to the birth of a new national feeling.

The Imperial Conference of 1897 was the first one in which a Canadian prime minister participated. At the time, the country did not control its foreign policy; Great Britain spoke on its behalf. The commander of the Canadian militia was a British officer, a situation that created a certain amount of friction. The fact that the prime minister of the young country was welcomed with so much consideration in London, and especially the fact that the English politicians and journalists were impressed by his elegance and his speeches, delighted his fellow citizens. "He put Canada before the British people, not as a sucking infant clinging to the Mother Country, but as a free, self-governing kingdom," said the journalist John Willison. The British fell under his spell. "Canada was held in high esteem, and next to the Queen, it was my husband who received the most applause," Zoé proudly related. "All along the route of the procession, all you heard was 'Canada!!' and 'Laurier!!'"

With members of the British government, Laurier used the strategy that had been so successful at home: he gave beautiful speeches that were tantalizingly ambiguous. He proclaimed his admiration for England, an admiration that, as we know, was genuine. He went so far as to say he was "British to the core." He seemed to open the door to the possibility of representation of the colonies at Westminster or in an eventual imperial forum, which was in keeping with the wishes of the British government: "It would be the proudest moment of my life if I could see a Canadian of French descent affirming the principles of freedom in the parliament of Great Britain."

Chamberlain was full of hope. Canada was the most populous and developed of the colonies and its support for the imperial plans would be decisive. He knew that if the colonies agreed to take part in an imperial council, they would be inextricably tied to policies decided by London. But he was soon disappointed. In the same speech, Laurier affirmed the growing autonomy of the colony he led: "Colonies are born to become nations.... The first place in our hearts is filled by Canada." And during the conference itself, he rejected the idea of forming a federal council. He was the one who drafted a motion in favour of the status quo for adoption by his colonial colleagues: "The relations between the United Kingdom and the self-governing colonies are generally satisfactory under the existing condition of things."

Unlike the local press, Chamberlain was not at all charmed. With each flight of lyricism by Laurier in favour of the Empire, he felt he was getting close to achieving his goal—only to discover that Laurier had no intention of going from words to concrete action. One of Chamberlain's biographers, Peter T. Marsh, describes how Laurier's style irritated the British statesman: "The ride with Laurier was all the more perplexing because he could make the lows seem so much like highs. Chamberlain and Laurier were masters of words. But whereas Chamberlain's words were noted for their clarity, Laurier used words evocatively."

Was Laurier an imperialist or a nationalist? An "intellectual imperialist" is how historian H. Blair Neatby sums him up, meaning that he believed in the political principles Great Britain had bequeathed to Canada and its other colonies. But beyond that, Laurier was certainly a Canadian nationalist. He knew that only national autonomy and the appeal to a shared Canadian pride and emotion could ensure the unity of the new country. On his return from the Jubilee conference, he was welcomed as a hero. On both banks of the Saint-Lawrence River, the residents lit bonfires. "He left the Prime Minister of a mere colony, and he returned the Prime Minister of an independent country," wrote the historian Robert Rumilly. "Today," Laurier told the crowds that came to cheer him, "Canada has taken its place among the nations of the world." He was not exaggerating; thanks to him, the country had begun its march toward full independence.

Laurier was to take part in three more Imperial Conferences (1902, 1907, and 1911). Each time, he would—politely—foil the plans of the English imperialists. Each time, he would return from London to be acclaimed by Canadians, who were increasingly conscious of their national identity.

Unfortunately, between conferences, events would sorely test Laurier's skills as a tightrope walker.

A WAR FOR GOLD

The first of these events occurred in October 1899, far from Ottawa and from London. In the South African province of Transvaal, English settlers were arriving in ever greater numbers, drawn by the discovery of large deposits of gold. Their presence was not welcomed by the Boers, descendants of the first white settlers, of Dutch, German, and French origin. The Transvaal government refused to give voting rights to the new settlers and levied unreasonable taxes on the English gold-mining industry. The mining companies demanded that the mother country intervene. War broke out, a typical imperialist war. Global security was certainly not at stake, and even less, Canada's security.

London nevertheless wanted the assistance of its colonies. It was not that Great Britain lacked the resources to fight the Boers. But in Chamberlain's mind, this was an ideal opportunity to strengthen the cohesion of the Empire in defence matters. Personally, Laurier was not inclined to send Canadian troops to the Transvaal; he did not see how the conflict was of concern to Canada. He did not, however, express this opinion clearly, probably for fear of offending the imperialists in the country. He preferred to emphasize the risk that a military adventure in South Africa would be too costly for the Canadian government: "We have a great deal to do in this country to develop it to its legitimate expansion. Military expenditure is of such a character that you never know where it will end," he wrote to Ontario journalist John Cameron. It was a pretext: if Laurier had been convinced that Ottawa should send troops to the Transvaal, the necessary funds would have been found.

Unlike the French Canadian elite, Laurier felt that London was right to want to bring the Boers in the Transvaal and the Orange Free State to heel. He had studied the issue carefully. To a priest who asked him not to support Chamberlain's policy, he gave a veritable history lesson on

South Africa and offered to send him "all the books on the history of the Boers and the current problems." His boundless admiration for British democracy prevented him from seeing the imperialist nature of the conflict. In addition, the Boers' decision to deprive the English settlers of the right to vote offended his liberalism. "There never was a juster war on the part of England than that war," he declared in the Commons.

Stirred up by the imperialists and their newspapers, Canadian anglophones enthusiastically adopted the cause of the uitlanders, or foreigners, in the Transvaal. The pressure on the government soon became irresistible. In the province of Quebec, on the other hand, the French Canadians were opposed to any participation in the conflict. They obviously did not feel the same attachment to the Empire as their compatriots. In addition, they were, as they would always be, for obvious reasons, sympathetic with the underdog. Even Laurier's friend Laurent-Olivier David, who could hardly be suspected of being a radical nationalist, had trouble accepting the idea that the government should send "a regiment to be decimated by bullets and disease in the Transvaal.... Confederation is bearing fruit. What will happen if ever a war breaks out between France and England. Damned Confederation!"

Another friend, Senator Raoul Dandurand, had a heated discussion with Laurier on the subject. Dandurand considered the war a "criminal assault on two small republics that [have] a right to their independence." He pointed out to Laurier that the British Liberal leader, Henry Campbell-Bannerman, was opposed to the British offensive, as was the rising star of the party, David Lloyd George. Laurier retorted: "Does it seem strange to you, as a person who loves France, that the English of this country love England? And if Canada, in which the majority is English, sent troops to Africa, in what way would your French dignity be injured, in what way would your French rights be attacked? Do you not believe, if you want to have allies on the day of battle, that it is good to respect the feelings of your allies?"

This disagreement between the two "races" led to deplorable racist comments, particularly in the English Canadian newspapers, which accused French Canadians of disloyalty and questioned the merits of preserving that distinct culture within the federation. As always, Laurier countered the strong emotions and narrow views on both sides with reason. He tried to find a middle course, based not on prejudices but on principles, his first principle being realism.

A compromise was finally reached: the government would equip those Canadians who wished to enlist as volunteers and send them to Africa, where they would be under the orders of British officers. The Cabinet's order-in-council stipulated that "such an expenditure cannot be ... construed as a precedent for future action." It was typical Laurier, full of ambiguity. In fact, for the first time, Canada was actually agreeing to take part in a war in which only the interests of the Empire and not those of the country were at stake. On this precise point, Henri Bourassa was correct: "The precedent is the fait accompli."

As we have already seen, the Cabinet's decision resulted in a break between Laurier and his protégé; Bourassa resigned as a member of Parliament, intending to win support for his position from the voters in Labelle in a by-election. "It is a question of deciding," he wrote to the prime minister, "if the Canadian people will be called upon to take part in all the wars of the Empire without the doors of the Cabinet and the imperial Parliament being opened to them, without even their representatives and their government being consulted on their participation in these bloody struggles." Bourassa was re-elected; Laurier wisely decided not to run a candidate against him.

Governing is the art of the possible. This was something Bourassa, the Cartesian-minded nationalist, failed to grasp. One cannot ignore the will of a large proportion of the population, unless that will would restrict the rights of the minority. And that was not the case here. By what logic would French Canadians have the right to prevent their volunteer compatriots from going to fight in South Africa, when that "does not attack either our rights or our honour or our dignity as a race"? wrote Laurier to a correspondent. "If we had refused our imperative duty," he declared in the House, "the most dangerous agitation would have arisen, an agitation which, according to all human probability, would have ended in a cleavage in the population of this country upon racial lines. A greater calamity could never take place in Canada."

A total of 7,300 Canadians, all volunteers, fought alongside the British in the Transvaal; 89 of them died in combat and 135 succumbed to diseases (especially typhoid fever) contracted in that inhospitable environment. French Canadians suffered no ill effects from that voluntary participation. There are even indications that some francophone Quebecers felt a certain pride in seeing so many brave Canadians go overseas. Willison recounted that on the day of departure of the first contingent from the port of Quebec City, there were many French speakers on the pier to send them off. In the election that came a few weeks after the government's decision, Laurier was returned to power, winning fifty-seven of the sixty-five seats in the province of Quebec. The discontent over the Boer War was apparently not great enough for francophones to turn against their leader. It must be said, however, that Quebec voters did not have much choice, since Tupper's Conservatives were even more imperialistic than the Liberals.

This being said, the debate on Canadian participation in the Transvaal conflict made Bourassa an important figure, the undisputed leader of the Quebec nationalists. And the gulf that had been opened between francophones and anglophones regarding Canada's role in times of war would never be bridged.

BETWEEN LONDON AND WASHINGTON

On March 30, 1867, three months before the coming into force of the British North America Act that created the Canadian federation, the American secretary of state, Frederick Seward, negotiated a treaty with Russia to purchase the vast wild territory of Alaska. As they struggled to recover from the Civil War, many Americans had trouble understanding the reason for this transaction of $7.2 million, a substantial sum at that time. Newspapers spoke of "Seward's folly" and "Seward's icebox."

The boundary between Alaska and British North

America had been established by a treaty signed by England and Russia four decades earlier. That text was imprecise in certain respects, but this was not of great concern since there was then little interest in those frozen lands. That indifference vanished with the Klondike Gold Rush, which began the year after Wilfrid Laurier became prime minister. Drawn by the promise of gold, thousands of Americans made the long journey to the Klondike, facing conditions they had not imagined in their worst nightmares. One of these adventurers, the writer Jack London, thus described the land: "A vast silence reigned over the territory. The land itself was a desolation, lifeless, without movement, so lone and cold that the spirit of it was not even that of sadness. There was a hint in it of laughter, but of a laughter more terrible than any sadness—a laughter that was mirthless as the smile of the Sphinx, a laughter cold as the frost and partaking of the grimness of infallibility. It was the masterful and incommunicable wisdom of eternity laughing at the futility of life and the effort of life. It was the Wild, the savage, frozen-hearted Northland Wild."

The Lynn Canal, a magnificent fjord that extends 140 kilometres northward, was the main access route to the trails to Yukon. It was precisely at this strip of coastline where the Alaskan Panhandle met northern British Columbia that the boundary had not been clearly drawn. The Americans claimed ownership of all the fjords along that part of the coast. Ottawa demanded that the boundary run to the west of the fjords, which would put them within Canadian territory. The American case appeared much more solid to many. Most maps of the period agreed with it. In addition, the Americans had been settling the region and had controlled it militarily for years. Nevertheless, the Canadian government insisted on claiming a slice of the pie.

Early in 1903, the Canadians and Americans agreed to submit the dispute to a tribunal of six "impartial jurists of repute." At the height of an American nationalism that considered the entire continent its exclusive zone of influence, the new president, the fiery Theodore Roosevelt, had no intention of giving an inch. He let the British government know that if the tribunal decided against him, he would ignore the decision and impose his views by force of arms if necessary. "The land in question is ours," declared the secretary of state, John Hay. "It was held by Russia in accordance with treaty from 1825 to 1867, and has been held by us ever since. We shall never think of giving it up. No administration could abandon it and live a minute."

Given the circumstances, Laurier had no illusions about the outcome of the matter. He quickly realized that

Roosevelt would play hardball, and he hoped at best to be able to save face. The three "jurists of repute" appointed by the president could in no way be considered objective; one was a member of the Roosevelt administration, and the other two were senators who had already expressed opinions hostile to the Canadian point of view. They were jurists, admittedly, but they were first of all politicians in the service of the president. Although he was furious, Laurier kept his side of the bargain and appointed two renowned jurists to the tribunal. The third member of the Canadian delegation was to be named by London; at Laurier's request, the British government chose the chief justice of the House of Lords, Lord Alverstone.

The tribunal studied the question and heard the parties for many weeks. From a legal perspective, the problem was complex. But the legal aspect did not really matter. The American representatives knew from the start what their decision would be. The same was true for the two Canadians. Laurier hoped that Lord Alverstone would support the Canadian side. That would mean a tie vote, a deadlock that would make it possible to extract concessions from the United States.

As the work of the tribunal progressed, the Canadian representatives increasingly had doubts about the neutrality of the English judge. When it was coming to an end, on October 8, 1903, the prime minister received the following cable from Clifford Sifton, who was in London to put forward his government's point of view: "I think that Chief Justice intends joining Americans deciding in such a way as to defeat us at every point. We all think that Chief Justice's intentions are unjustifiable and due to predetermination to avoid trouble with United States." Indeed, the English were determined to preserve good relations with the United States; they were not about to let such a trivial issue spoil their efforts.

The Canadian delegates considered withdrawing from the tribunal in protest. Despite his anger, the prime minister rejected the idea. Instead, he asked them to threaten the British: "If we are thrown over by Chief Justice, he will give the last blow to British diplomacy in Canada. He should be plainly told this by our Commissioners." The English government was therefore caught between two threats, that of Roosevelt and that of Laurier. The first threat was obviously of greater concern. Ten days later, Lord Alverstone voted in favour of the Americans, and the tribunal granted the United States control of the fjords, in particular the Lynn Canal. "The completeness of the victory is amazing," gloated the secretary of state. Alverstone had clearly made an agreement with the American representatives, and he refused to even give Canada the consolation prize Laurier had hoped for, control over access to the Portland Canal at the southern end of the disputed territory. Laurier thus obtained nothing that would allow him to claim that he had extracted some concession from the Americans.

Held responsible for this humiliation by the Conservative Opposition, Laurier was enraged. "I have often regretted that while they [the U.S.] are a great and powerful nation, we are only a small colony, a growing colony, but still a colony," he said in the House. "I have often regretted also that we have not in our own hands the treaty-making power which would enable us to dispose of our own affairs.... So long as Canada remains a dependency of the British Crown the present powers that we have are not sufficient for the maintenance of our rights. It is important that we should ask the British parliament for more extensive powers so that if ever we have to deal with matters of a similar nature again, we shall deal with them in our own way, in our own fashion, according to the best light that we have."

We do not know if Laurier's irritation was genuine or if he was only trying to blame the British for his failure. Perhaps he wanted to keep Canadians from coming to a conclusion that went against the nationalist optimism he was trying to instill: their country was quite simply too weak to make its influence felt on Great Britain and the United States. One thing is certain: this matter provoked unprecedented indignation in Canada, indignation that was aimed more at the English than at the Americans. "Nothing is surer than that Canada has suffered incalculable loss and despoilment through the dealings of British diplomatists with Canadian interests and Canadian territory," said the *News* of Toronto. The *Globe* declared, "The feeling is strongest in those who stand firmer than ever against annexation, and who are not disposed towards independence. Because they are 'Sons of the Blood' they resent injustice, even from Britain." Never since the birth of Confederation had national feeling been expressed with such force. Canadians realized that when it had to choose, the United Kingdom would not hesitate to sacrifice the interests of a colony for its own.

The only politician who kept his composure in this debate was ... Henri Bourassa! Who would have thought it? Bourassa had studied the documents closely and concluded that the Canadian case was doomed from the outset. "Perhaps it would be well for the Canadian people to acknowledge the facts before they indulge in such wild talk as we have seen in some of the newspapers," he said. And he summed up the situation perfectly: "We must come to the conclusion that if Lord Alverstone acted strictly according to his judicial functions in regard to the former and most important question [the ownership of the fjords], in regard to the latter question [the ownership of the islands at the mouth of Portland Canal], he played the role of a diplomat rather than that of a judge."

After the prime minister's declarations in the House of Commons, we would have expected him to undertake formal procedures to obtain for the Dominion the right to negotiate and sign its own treaties. He did nothing of the kind. His first biographer, Oscar Skelton, who knew him well and who later became undersecretary of state for foreign affairs, explained that "nothing was more foreign to Sir Wilfrid's ruling bias than to urge any policy on general and theoretical grounds; not until a concrete issue arose would the demand for wider powers be renewed."

It was thus in small steps that Canada would become autonomous in the area of foreign affairs. Autonomy by stealth was Laurier's strategy. In 1907, four years after the tribunal's decision on the Alaska boundary dispute, a representative of Canada, the minister Rodolphe Lemieux, concluded an agreement with the government of Japan under which it would limit emigration of its nationals to

Canada. It was the first agreement the Canadian government negotiated and signed on its own behalf.

Although Canadian politicians at the turn of the century had ambitions of playing a wider role on the international stage, they did not have the necessary bureaucracy. The undersecretary of state, Joseph Pope, complained constantly about the lack of a system for archiving the numerous documents from diplomatic exchanges. He suggested to Laurier that he create a secretariat of external affairs. (The term *foreign affairs* was avoided, since London was jealous of its predominant role in this domain.) Ever prudent, Laurier did not rush things. Finally, in 1909, he tabled the bill to create the new department. Strangely enough, although this was a crucial step toward the country's autonomy, there was no significant debate on the bill. The prime minister did everything he could to reassure London and the imperialists, arguing that "it is not intended it shall be a very numerous department, a very heavy department." At the same time, he resisted pressure from Pope and the Governor General, Lord Grey, who wanted the wording of the bill to define the limits of the new department's scope of action. He made no grand statements, but he stubbornly refused to restrict future possibilities. The foundations were laid for a distinctive Canadian foreign policy.

TROUBLED WATERS

During the same period, the Royal Navy saw its domination of the seas disputed by another power for the first time in two hundred years. In 1898, the German kaiser Wilhelm II launched an ambitious shipbuilding program. In the years that followed, this program caused increasing concern, even panic, in British military and political circles. In Parliament on March 16, 1909, the First Lord of the Admiralty, Reginald McKenna, revealed that the Germans had made astounding progress and their shipbuilding capacity was now equal to that of the United Kingdom. The Liberal government of Herbert Asquith, which had not been much inclined to spend money on weapons, was persuaded to announce the construction of eight dreadnought-class battleships, the most advanced warships of their time. "No matter what the cost, the safety of the country must be assured," McKenna declared.

In Canada, the imperialists hastened to demand that the government make a special contribution to London's efforts in the form of either money or dreadnoughts. In the province of Quebec, Bourassa's nationalists felt, on the contrary, that Canada had no interest in contributing to the imperialist policy, and that any contribution would automatically involve the country in conflicts that had more to do with British appetites than its own interests. So, ten years after the beginning of the Boer War, there was a new controversy related to the defence of the Empire, with the same main actors and arguments. Once again, Laurier defined a middle course that he defended with beautiful words and ambiguity. Once again, the extremists on both sides joined forces against him.

Rather than give money or ships to Great Britain, Laurier proposed to provide Canada with its own navy. A few years earlier, the Department of Marine and Fisheries had purchased two new ships to patrol Canadian waters. These first armed ships enabled Canadians to take part in manoeuvres with the British Navy. They were quickly considered warships, the nucleus of the country's future navy. Quebecers were able to admire one of these ships, the *Canada*, alongside the newest and most powerful of the British warships, the *Indomitable*, during a big naval gathering organized for the tercentenary of Quebec City in 1908.

The navy announced by Laurier was to be used first and foremost to protect the country's coasts. In times of necessity, it could be placed under the control of the imperial fleet. It was a shrewd move to call on the nascent Canadian nationalism to argue that as an increasingly autonomous nation, Canada should have its own navy, which it would then be free to contribute to the service of the Empire.

Like any compromise—and this is the tragedy of Laurier's life—it was savagely attacked. The imperialists ridiculed the "tin-pot navy" proposed by the government. To them, Canada had no need for an autonomous navy, and it was the supremacy of the great imperial fleet that must be assured. The Quebec nationalists also rejected the government plan. In Bourassa's view, the creation of a Canadian navy would lead not only to Canada's participation in imperial wars but to conscription, a terrifying thought in Quebec. The virulence of the nationalist campaign against Laurier was unprecedented. Bourassa said at an assembly in Saint-Eustache: "I say that when a man, whatever his personal qualities, shows such contempt for the trust and love a people has given him as to betray his own people in one action, I say that such a man is more dangerous to his faith, to his country, and even to the British Crown than the worst of the Orangemen."

Laurier explained his position brilliantly throughout this fierce debate. His pragmatism was as always embellished by his mastery of the art of oratory. On one occasion, he made a controversial declaration: "When Great Britain is at war, Canada is at war." These few words aroused strong feelings among the Quebec nationalists. A few weeks later, Laurier qualified his views, saying that he had merely stated a principle of international law: "If England is at war we are at war and liable to attack. I do not say that we shall always be attacked, neither do I say that we would take part in all the wars of England. That is a matter that must be guided by circumstances, upon which the Canadian parliament will have to pronounce, and will have to decide in its own best judgment."

What are we to conclude from this? That, unlike many of his French Canadian fellow citizens, the prime minister was aware of reality, domestic political reality and international geopolitical reality. Canada was part of an empire. Its growing autonomy entitled it to a certain freedom of action, of course, but when the higher interests of the Empire were at stake, Canada would have to stand beside England. Moreover, Laurier was convinced, this was in the best interest of Canada and of civilization.

CHAPTER 6

The Century

> The nineteenth century was the century of the United
> States. I think we can claim that it is Canada that shall fill
> the twentieth century.
> **WILFRID LAURIER, 1904**

The epigraph to this chapter is the best-known quotation
from Wilfrid Laurier. This is rather paradoxical, because the
prophecy is simply mistaken. Canada certainly had an
extraordinary twentieth century, becoming a modern, prosperous country, but was it ever a great power in the making,
as the United States of the nineteenth century was? Even at
the time he spoke these words, Laurier had little reason to
believe his vision would become a reality. The unbridled
optimism of his words can only be attributed to the
demands of partisan politics.

It is true that the beginning of the twentieth century was
a time of optimism in Canada. After its first unsure steps,
the country was taking shape. The construction of the
transcontinental railway under Macdonald had opened the
way for the settlement of the West. The economy was

becoming industrialized, first under Macdonald and his National Policy and even more under Laurier. The country was discovering the wealth of its natural resources, especially its minerals. In the West, the wheat economy was thriving. Everything seemed possible. Canadian nationalism was taking its place alongside attachment to the Empire. But to say that Canada—with five million inhabitants—would one day be more populous than Great Britain, with forty million, and the United States, with eighty million, as Laurier predicted, was not realistic. However, in 1904, with the approach of a general election, realism was easily forgotten.

GO WEST, YOUNG FOREIGNER

If the Laurier years were so prosperous, it was first of all because the Liberals were lucky to have come into power when the world was climbing out of the Long Depression (1873–1896). Demand for raw materials was increasing, and hundreds of thousands of Europeans were ready to do anything, even to cross the Atlantic and settle in the middle of nowhere, in the hope of escaping poverty. The Laurier government also benefited from the actions of its Conservative predecessor in building the Canadian Pacific Railway and putting down the rebellions in the West. The vast prairies of the West were therefore open to anyone willing to break the sod with a plough. All that was needed for thousands of foreigners to come and settle the land was a well-defined immigration policy guided by a determined minister. Laurier found such a minister in the person of Clifford Sifton.

As attorney general in the Manitoba government of Thomas Greenway, Sifton had impressed the prime minister with his intellectual abilities and his energy. He had no trouble convincing Laurier that agricultural immigration was the key to Canada's future. Was it to guide that policy that Laurier brought him into his Cabinet? There is no indication that Laurier took a particular interest in immigration, or in economic questions in general except insofar as they could help or hinder the electoral prospects of his party. It was mostly for strategic reasons that Laurier recruited Sifton: he was counting on the young minister—who was thirty-five years old—to provide the Liberal Party with a solid organization in the West.

When Laurier took power, Canada was receiving barely fifteen to twenty thousand immigrants a year. This increase in population, however, was cancelled out by the exodus of thousands to the United States. To populate the West, Sifton established an aggressive immigration system based on bonuses paid to European agents according to the number of immigrants they persuaded to set sail for Canada. As minister of the interior, he also worked hard to entice Canadians who had settled in the United States to come back, and many of them did. The number of immigrants went from 17,000 in 1896 to 331,000 in 1911, Laurier's last year in power, which is 70,000 more immigrants than the country accepts annually now.

The majority of the new citizens came from the United States and the British Isles. Thousands more came from various European countries—Russia, Poland, Germany, Austria—that Sifton had identified as the most likely to provide the sturdy farmers he was looking for. He chose well: agricultural production soared. From 1900 to 1910, exports of wheat out of the port of Montreal tripled, going from four million to fourteen million bushels. Sheltered by the tariffs of Macdonald's National Policy, the manufacturing economy in the centre of the country benefited from the huge expansion of the West.

The large wave of immigration was not without significant problems. First, there was strong concern among Canadians of British descent, who were displeased that all these people from foreign cultures were settling among them. The editor of the *Canadian Magazine* wrote: "Mr. Sifton is doing clever work, but his policy is a mistaken one. The immigrants he is securing are not so desirable as those from the British Isles. They are rude, barbarous and uncultured. We do not want slaves, we want men." Appeals for a policy of assimilation became increasingly insistent. Hence the importance anglophone Canadians placed on the establishment of a single school system, which they saw as the only way of creating a united nation. As we saw above, the francophones of the West were collateral victims of this policy.

French Canadians had an additional reason for being concerned about the demographic evolution of the country. Among the tens of thousands of immigrants settling in Canada, very few spoke French. The proportion of francophones in the country was thus being reduced year by year. Armand Lavergne and Henri Bourassa accused the federal government of not making enough effort to recruit new Canadians from France and Belgium. "I protest the conspiration against French immigration which is carried on in the Interior Department," said Lavergne during a debate on immigration in the House of Commons in 1907. "The motto of the Immigration Department seems to have been: the Doukhobors rather than the French." The minister, Rodolphe Lemieux, rejected the accusation, saying that "this government is doing its level best to bring out the French settlers to this country." But, he pointed out with good reason, "the [French] people will stay in France and the French government will see that its own population does not emigrate."

Although there indeed were immigration agents in France and Belgium, the resources in place did not compare to those devoted to attracting British and other Europeans. Ottawa felt that, given the limited success of its efforts in those two francophone countries, it would be a waste of public funds to invest more. The nationalists replied that if the federal government did more, the number of immigrants from France and Belgium would be greater. Speaking of the French, Armand Lavergne argued that "they would be willing to come to Canada if a wise propaganda were carried amongst them," pretending not to be aware of the French government's opposition to emigration.

What did Laurier think of all this? Two months after he came to power in June 1896, he received a letter and a memorandum from Paul Wiallard, a Frenchman who had settled in Canada and had for a few years been promoting French emigration to British North America. Wiallard noted the disparity between the resources devoted to attracting immigrants from continental Europe and those invested in attracting immigrants from the British Isles. He suggested that a permanent agency be created on the Continent that would be responsible for recruiting immigrants from France, Belgium, Switzerland, Luxembourg, and Italy. And he offered his services. Laurier was thus well aware of the problem. He even received a letter from a farmer in the north of France who asked him, as a condition for his coming to Canada, for the loan of a thousand sheep! But the prime minister did not seem concerned about the low proportion of francophone immigrants settling in the West. When asked about the issue, he lamented the fact that French Canadians seeking a better life preferred the United States to the Canadian territories: "I would have wanted emigration from Canada, from the province of Quebec, to have gone toward the Western provinces instead of to the United States. There are a million Canadians in the United States; they should be in the new provinces."

It was only in 1903 that the persistent Wiallard saw his wishes fulfilled; he was appointed immigration agent in Paris at the suggestion of Senator Raoul Dandurand, who was worried by the success of the nationalist discourse on immigration in Quebec. At Wiallard's insistence, the Canadian agency in Paris redoubled its efforts to recruit French immigrants. But this aroused the ire of the French government. None other than Georges Clemenceau, the French prime minister, published a circular with the unequivocal title

"Contre l'émigration au Canada" (Against emigration to Canada), in which he stressed the difficulties encountered by Frenchmen who had been lured by the wide-open spaces of Canada. He instructed French civil servants "to strive, by advising them at every possible opportunity, to dissuade our compatriots from their rash plans to settle in Canada." The Belgian government was less hostile to emigration than that of France, but it still warned those who were tempted by the adventure against the overly optimistic Canadian propaganda.

The combined efforts of the governments of Canada and the province of Quebec nevertheless had some effect. From 1901 to 1911, the number of French nationals living in Canada went from eight thousand to more than seventeen thousand, while the number of Belgians went from a little more than two thousand to eight thousand. But those numbers were ridiculously small compared to the total of nine hundred thousand foreigners who were added to the Canadian population over that decade. At the beginning of the twentieth century, France and Belgium provided six times fewer immigrants than Russia and Poland.

After their victory in the 1911 election, thanks to help from Bourassa's disciples, Borden's Conservatives sent the nationalist journalist Olivar Asselin to investigate the situation in France and Belgium. There he observed the meagre resources available to the Canadian representatives. He deplored the fact that "it is customary to answer people in English when they directly address the Department of the Interior in French, Flemish or Dutch to request information about Canada." He admitted, however, that Paris had strongly expressed its displeasure with the propaganda of the Canadian agents; he therefore felt that Belgium offered greater potential in the short term. Finally, he was sure that "with a good placement system, Canada could recruit annually, in Belgium alone, thousands of farm workers capable, for the most part, of themselves founding farms after very little time." But the Conservative government did not obtain better results than Laurier's had. In 1921, there were in the country 369,000 more people born abroad than there had been ten years earlier, and only 7,000 of them had come from France or Belgium.

LAURIER GOES OFF THE RAILS

The phenomenal growth of the West, the prevailing optimism, and political considerations had led Laurier to decree that the twentieth century would be Canada's century. The same factors would lead him to much more imprudent action: the construction, at great expense to the public treasury and with grossly deficient planning, of a second transcontinental railway.

At the beginning of the century, everyone agreed that the Canadian Pacific Railway was no longer sufficient. The population in the West had increased faster than expected, and there had been exponential growth in agriculture and manufacturing, the products of which had to be transported by rail. In the Prairies, farmers were furious with the CPR for abusing its monopoly by charging unreasonable rates. Clearly, new rail lines had to be built. While this was widely acknowledged, the solutions proposed varied greatly. Everyone—ministers, promoters, local lobbies—had their own ideas, routes, and plans. William Mackenzie and Donald Mann, founders of the Canadian Northern Railway, a regional line in the West, dreamed of connecting Vancouver to Montreal following a route about three hundred kilometres north of the Canadian Pacific line. The general manager of the Grand Trunk Railway, the American Charles Hays, had ambitions of making his own network, concentrated in eastern Canada and the American northeast, a transcontinental line.

The adventure of the Canadian Pacific should have taught Laurier that before going ahead with such an ambitious project, careful planning was essential. Hadn't the

Liberals criticized Macdonald twenty years before for embarking on the construction of the Canadian Pacific without taking into account the needs and financial resources of the country? "I have never heard expressed here the opinion that the Canadian Pacific Railway should not be built, but the policy of the Liberals is that it should be built gradually as the wants of the country require and its resources permit," Laurier had declared in the House during the debate on the CPR. But the prudence he had recommended to the Conservative government at that time was forgotten in 1903 when it came time for him to launch his own transcontinental railway project.

Clifford Sifton recommended that the prime minister set up a commission of experts. But Laurier was not interested in experts' advice. Sifton felt that the only way to ensure the profitability of a second transcontinental railway was to force an alliance between the Canadian Northern and the Grand Trunk railways. Laurier tried to act as mediator between the two, but they were both set on their ambitions and were not interested; he did not have the will to impose the only sensible solution.

An election was coming up, and Laurier wanted his project of the century off the ground at all costs. It was also important to him to satisfy the voters in Ontario, Quebec,

THE CENTURY

and the Maritimes who were demanding that the railway—
modernity!—come to their town or city. This was the case
for Quebec City, which was represented in the House of
Commons by the prime minister himself, and which wanted
to be able to compete with Montreal as a port of transit to
the Atlantic Ocean. So, instead of the rational plan Sifton
wanted, Laurier adopted a short-sighted approach dominated by partisan interests and nationalist theatrics. Despite his
acknowledged lack of expertise in economic and financial
questions, he took personal charge of the dossier, shutting
out his minister of railways, Andrew Blair. As was increasingly the case in his administration, the prime minister did
as he pleased. He wanted absolutely, it was said, to avoid his
government's being caught up in a new Canadian Pacific
scandal. There would be no scandal of that kind—but there
would be a scandal.

On July 30, 1903, Laurier presented his plan to
Parliament. The solution that had been negotiated was complex. The western portion of the new railway—between
Winnipeg and Prince Rupert—would be built by a new subsidiary of the Grand Trunk, the Grand Trunk Pacific, which
would be its owner. The financing of the project would be
backed by government guarantees. The Grand Trunk would
also build the eastern portion—between Moncton and

Winnipeg—but this segment would belong to the government, which would lease it to the Grand Trunk Pacific. Laurier defended his project with his usual eloquence. His words contrasted sharply with what he had said to Macdonald two decades earlier. Then, as we have seen, he accused the government of rushing things; now he was claiming that no time should be lost: "To those who urge upon us the policy of tomorrow and tomorrow and tomorrow; to those who tell us wait, wait, wait; to those who advise us to pause, to consider, to reflect, to calculate and to inquire, our answer is: No, this is not a time for deliberation, this is a time for action.… Heaven grant that it is not already too late; Heaven grant that, while we tarry and dispute, the trade of Canada is not deviated to other channels and that an ever-vigilant competitor does not take to himself the trade that properly belongs to those who acknowledge Canada as their native or their adopted land."

It was not so much the complexity of the arrangement with Grand Trunk that doomed the new transcontinental rail line, but its route, which was based on incomplete data and partisan considerations. It was also Mackenzie and Mann's obstinate determination to build their own national railway—which was predictable to anyone who knew them. The eastern portion of the new transcontinental route was to go through northern Quebec and Ontario, territory that was sparsely populated, difficult, and unfamiliar. This decision not only generated unforeseen costs but guaranteed that the enterprise would never be viable.

Laurier had planned on the construction of the eastern portion of the railway costing $13 million. The contract stipulated a rent of 3 percent of the construction costs; Grand Trunk thus expected to pay around $400,000 a year. But the project finally cost $170 million, thirteen times more than expected! Grand Trunk's calculations no longer held; this section would never be profitable. According to the Royal Commission of Inquiry that examined the ballooning costs, half of the unforeseen expenses—close to $70 million—was due to theft and waste.

In the West, the Grand Trunk Pacific built a high-quality railway at a much more reasonable cost. Nevertheless, the country ended up with three railways between Winnipeg and the Pacific, two of which, the Canadian Northern and the Grand Trunk Pacific, followed essentially the same route as far as the Rockies. Once again, commercial failure was guaranteed. As a result, in the East as well as the West, Laurier's railway would collapse under debt. After the Great War, the Borden government would have no choice but to nationalize the Grand Trunk, its subsidiary the Grand Trunk Pacific, the

National Transcontinental, the Intercolonial in the Maritimes, and the Canadian Northern. Thus was born Canadian National Railway.

The fragility of Laurier's project and the incompetence of those responsible were tragically symbolized by the collapse (the first of two) of the Quebec City bridge under construction in 1907. This tragedy, which was attributed to the negligence of the engineers involved, cost the lives of seventy-five workers. To the *Quebec Chronicle*, this was "one of the worst disasters in the ancient capital's history." It described the scene: "Today all that remains of the massive and stupendous undertaking is a tangle of twisted and broken steel work, jumbled into a mass of ruin, almost beyond credibility." The blow was all the harder for Laurier because he himself had laid the first stone in a grandiose ceremony seven years earlier. He spoke of the accident as a "national calamity."

The talents that had served Laurier so well throughout his political career were of no help to him in this complex matter, which pitted multiple financial, economic, and political interests against each other and involved many technical issues. Rather, it required a clear, meticulously prepared plan and an unshakable determination to carry it through. The art of compromise, the desire to please everyone for personal as well as political reasons, and the genius for letting himself "float in the ambient air," so dear to Laurier, inevitably resulted in a disproportionate and incoherent project. Even the great man's silver tongue could not cover up this gigantic failure.

THE NEIGHBOURS TO THE SOUTH

There is nothing new about the ambivalent feelings Canadians have toward their neighbours to the south. This love–hate relationship was already well established when Laurier began his political career. At the time, Canadians had good reason to fear that the United States would try to annex the huge territories north of the border. The War of 1812 was still fresh in their memory. In addition, it was not unusual for American politicians to speak of the day when the star-spangled banner would fly over all of America north of Mexico.

The outbreak of the Civil War (1861–1865) revealed a country that was deeply divided and unstable, and whose model of government and society Canadians certainly would not want to see established here; indeed, that tragedy provided a powerful impetus to the plans to unite the British colonies of North America. Many citizens of the new federation were descendants of people who had fled the United

States after the War of Independence, and this contributed to the feeling of suspicion toward Canada's hyperactive neighbour. At the same time, the United States was attractive: as we have seen, the flow of Canadians leaving their country to take advantage of the prosperity to the south was constantly growing.

Sir Wilfrid shared some of his fellow citizens' reservations with regard to the United States. In the debate on the Autonomy Bills in 1905, he emphasized the advantages of teaching students religion, in contrast to practices south of the border: "When I observe in this country of ours a total absence of lynchings and an almost total absence of divorces and murders, for my part, I thank heaven that we are living in a country where the young children of the land are taught Christian morals and Christian dogmas." This being said, he showed no hint of exaggerated fear or hostility with regard to the United States. On several occasions, he went there to convalesce. And as I have mentioned, he was an unconditional admirer of Abraham Lincoln, "one of the greatest men of history." Contemporaries have said that he had read everything written about him, and that he considered the Gettysburg Address ("Four score and seven years ago our fathers brought forth on this continent a new nation ...") and his second inaugural address ("but let us judge not, that we be not judged") classics. In a lecture he gave in Montreal in 1909, where he had been asked to make a comparison of the British and American constitutions, he demonstrated extensive knowledge of the American political system and the people working in it. He described the United States as "so united, so strong, so proud—so legitimately proud—of its glorious past and its colossal future."

Laurier knew that the future of Canada would in large part be determined by the evolution of its relationship with the United States. He therefore devoted a lot of time to this question, in particular to strengthening trade between the two countries. However, it is not easy to follow his intellectual process on the subject. Before he came to power, his declarations were often ambiguous. He seemed to be feeling his way, floating trial balloons. The following was a typical pronouncement: "I am not ready for my part to say that commercial union should be adopted at the present moment. A great deal of study and reflection are needed to solve this question, for and against which there is much to be said. The commercial union idea may be realized, and it may also be surrounded by insurmountable difficulties."

It is true that it was a sensitive question. As Liberal leader, Laurier had to distinguish himself from his Conservative adversaries, the fathers of the National Policy, which

involved high tariffs to protect fledgling Canadian industries. He also had to avoid arousing the Loyalist sentiments
that Macdonald was so capable of using to his advantage.

Philosophically, Laurier was probably in favour of the
greatest freedom of trade possible. However, we know that
he was the most pragmatic of men. In 1876, when he was a
young MP in the government of Alexander Mackenzie
(1873–1878), he defined himself as a "moderate protection-
ist." He felt that protecting Canadian industries was "a matter of necessity for a young nation, in order that it may attain
the full development of its own resources. If I were in Britain
I would avow free trade, but I am a Canadian born and res-
ident, and I think that we require protection. But to what
extent do we need it? I consider that the present tariff affords
sufficient protection."

The Mackenzie government lasted only one term; in
1878, Macdonald was returned to power, where he would
remain for a long time. In 1887, Sir John A. once again beat
the Liberals, this time led by Edward Blake. Despite Blake's
protests that he did not want to modify the tariffs of the
National Policy, the Conservatives had campaigned against
the Liberals' alleged support of free trade. The trade issue
had become a hot potato for the Liberal Party.

When he took the reins of the party a few months later,

Laurier needed to redefine the Liberal policy on trade. Surprisingly, in view of what had happened to his predecessor, he was attracted by the idea of a commercial union with the United States. His reasons seem to have been essentially tactical: "We must try to make a new departure," he wrote to Blake. "There is a universal desire for change. Commercial union would afford relief and commercial union must be popular. It is the general desire that we should make it a party issue." To Laurier's great regret, the subject divided the two; Blake was convinced that commercial union would necessarily lead to political union. In spite of his admiration for his former leader, Laurier ignored Blake's opposition; he wanted to put his own stamp on the party whose leadership had fallen to him without his seeking it and without his having much solid support.

While this bold policy had some supporters in the Liberal Party, it had more opponents. The Liberals knew how electorally vulnerable any policy of rapprochement with the United States made them. They wanted to lower tariffs, of course, but a commercial union, with the elimination of customs posts on the border and shared external tariffs that it implied, would be political suicide. Laurier was apparently too inexperienced to realize this right away. The English member of Parliament Joseph Chamberlain took it upon himself to stir up the Canadian imperialists: if Canada were to conclude a commercial union with the United States, he said, it would mean "political separation from Great Britain."

Laurier had to face facts; the idea of a commercial union gave way to the less compromising one of "unrestricted reciprocity." Raw materials, agricultural products, and manufactured goods would move freely between the two countries, but each one would maintain control of its tariff policy with respect to the rest of the world, and the customs posts would remain in place. Liberal MP Richard Cartwright tabled a motion to this effect in the House of Commons in March 1888. In his speech in support of the motion, Laurier presented his vision of the situation, which, as always, was idealistic: "Under the penetrating influence of discussions, of better feelings on both sides of the line, the hostility which now stains our long frontier will disappear, the barriers which now obstruct trade will burst open, and trade will pour in along all the avenues from the north to the south and from the south to the north, free, untrammelled and no longer stained by the hues of hostility."

That vision was not embraced by the Conservatives. They set out to demonstrate that unrestricted reciprocity would lead inevitably to commercial union, which would result just as inevitably in annexation. As he had four years earlier, Macdonald delighted in making this the main theme of the 1891 election campaign, Laurier's first one as leader. The old lion thundered: "A British subject I was born, a British subject I will die. With my utmost effort, with my latest breath, will I oppose the 'veiled treason' which attempts, by sordid means and mercenary proffers, to lure our people from their allegiance." We can easily imagine the impact of such a speech on Canadians of British origin. The Conservatives were re-elected, although with a reduced majority.

If the idea of free trade had merely been a tactical expedient, Laurier would then have abandoned it once and for all. Why should he persist in defending a policy that left him so open to attacks by his adversaries? And yet, persist he did. In 1893, the party congress approved the concept of a "fair and liberal reciprocity treaty" between Canada and the United States. It was no longer a question of a commercial union or of unrestricted reciprocity, but the idea of strengthening trade ties with our neighbours remained.

To the delight of the Liberals, the issue suddenly became less controversial. There were many reasons for this, but the main one was that American interest in a free trade treaty was fading. In 1890, Washington had established the

McKinley Tariffs, which imposed duties of nearly 50 percent on imported goods, including agricultural products. In 1894, the father of these tariffs, William McKinley, was elected president of the United States. The possibility of a trade treaty between the two countries seemed more remote than ever.

The Liberals themselves no longer wasted their energy on it. When they came to power in 1896, they tabled a budget that maintained the tariffs of the National Policy, except for goods imported not from the United States but from Great Britain. Unexpectedly, the latter were to benefit from lower duties. What was the reason for such an about-face? The journalist John Willison, Laurier's contemporary, who followed these questions closely, felt that the motives were purely political: "Consummate politician as he was he must at once have seen its advantages as he enjoyed the situation which actual presentation of the proposal created among his opponents in parliament." The imperialists, who had dreaded the Liberals' policy on trade, were surprised to find themselves applauding the new government. All the same, in the area of trade, geography trumped politics: during Laurier's tenure in office, imports from the United Kingdom would triple, while those from our neighbours to the south would increase fivefold.

Laurier continued to hope that one day it would be possible to work things out with the Americans. He was right. That day would come fourteen years later. In the spring of 1910, when he was finishing his fourth term and his administration was showing increasing signs that it was running out of steam, Washington threw him a lifeline. The Republican president, William H. Taft, proposed that they open negotiations on the liberalization of trade between the two countries: "I am profoundly convinced that these two countries, touching each other for more than three thousand miles, have common interests in trade and require special arrangements in legislation and administration which are not involved in the relations of the United States with countries beyond the seas." It was a lifeline not only for Laurier but also for Taft, who was in great difficulty although he had been in office only for a year. Having promised to reduce a large number of tariffs, he was unable to persuade Congress to adopt a bill to that effect, even though it was controlled by his party. On the contrary, the Payne-Aldrych Law promised to lower tariffs on 650 products and to increase duties on more than 200. This flawed compromise succeeded in making both proponents and opponents of tariff decreases unhappy. Therefore, in 1910, Wilfrid Laurier and William Taft were two anxious men in search of a new policy that would revive their respective administrations. They hoped reciprocity would achieve this. Formal negotiations began in October 1910. They progressed rapidly, and resulted in an agreement in January 1911.

In Canada, the gulf between Conservatives and Liberals on trade issues was never as great as it seemed in the speeches made during election campaigns. Even under John A. Macdonald, Canada had been interested in increasing its trade with the United States. Like the Grits, the Tories were under pressure from farmers, who dreamed of finding outlets for their growing production in the huge American market. The Conservatives were therefore favourable to the elimination of tariffs on agricultural products, but they insisted on continuing to protect manufactured goods. The Macdonald government had made overtures to Washington on this, but without success. The agreement concluded in 1911 by the Taft and Laurier administrations was in keeping with that approach. "We have gone very cautiously, with great care into this agreement," explained Laurier. The results were spectacular: customs duties on natural products—food, timber, metals—were eliminated or substantially reduced, while tariffs remained substantial on manufactured goods. In short, farmers would have full access to the American market, while Canadian industry would still be protected.

Politically, it was a master stroke, although the credit for it goes less to Laurier than to the political context in the United States. When the details of the agreement were announced in the House of Commons by the minister of finance, William Fielding, on January 26, 1911, the Conservatives were in despair. "There was the deepest dejection in our party, and many of our members were confident that the government's proposals would appeal to the country and would give it another term of office," wrote the Tory leader, Robert Borden, in his memoirs.

However, the Liberals made a serious strategic error. They should have taken advantage of Conservative disarray to call an early general election, especially since Borden was at this time the target of an attempted putsch in his party. By delaying, the government gave the Opposition time to recover and go on the offensive. In the House of Commons the Tories dragged things out, preventing the quick adoption of the bill implementing the Laurier–Taft agreement. It was a brilliant tactic: in May, the prime minister had to leave the country for two months to attend the Imperial Conference and the coronation of George V. Borden used those two months to mount a vigorous campaign against the agreement. The Conservatives fell back on Macdonald's tried-and-true strategy, arguing that reciprocity would weaken ties with the

Empire and lead to the annexation of Canada by the United States. It did not matter that, as Laurier reminded them, the provisions of the agreement were exactly those Macdonald himself had wanted to negotiate with the United States.

Both sides used extraordinary means to persuade Canadians. The government distributed advertising in favour of reciprocity through postmasters and census takers. Its opponents, enjoying substantial financial resources, used them to publish articles supporting their position in every newspaper in the country.

Laurier did not have to fight only the Conservative Party. The powerful manufacturing and railway industries were also hostile to reciprocity. A group of eighteen businessmen from Ontario, all Liberals, published a manifesto arguing that reciprocity "would weaken the ties that bind Canada to the Empire and make it more difficult to avert political union with the United States." The former president of the Canadian Pacific, the formidable William Van Horne, announced that he "was out to bust the damned thing." The economist and satirist Stephen Leacock, a fervent imperialist, added his influential two cents: "The Americans are a great people, but fifty years ago we settled the question as to what our lot was to be with respect to them. We have decided once and for all that the British flag was good enough for us."

Paradoxically, the Liberal Party aroused against itself not only imperialist sentiments but the budding Canadian nationalism of which Laurier himself had been the most effective inspiration. According to Borden, the trade agreement would work against the national economy Canadians had built since Confederation: "Loyalty to their memory and to the ideals which they consecrated demands that we should continue with firm heart and unabated hope upon the path which we entered nearly fifty years ago."

Laurier's former strongman in the West, Clifford Sifton, once favourable to reciprocity, had switched sides and was campaigning against the agreement with Washington. "Why?" Laurier asked him. "Because I do not believe in it," he replied. "You did once." "Yes, but conditions have changed." "No, it is you who have changed." Whatever the reasons for Sifton's change of heart, his campaign had a considerable impact. To him, he argued, the agreement "binds British Columbia to Oregon and to Washington and to California; it binds provinces of the Northwest to the states immediately to the south of them; it binds Ontario and Québec to the states south of us, and it binds the Maritime provinces to the states of New England." If Canadians turned toward their American neighbours too much, wouldn't the dream of a Canada from sea to sea inexorably fade away?

Never lacking for a grandiose vision, Laurier felt, on the contrary, that closer north–south trade ties would be good not only for both countries but for the world: "There may be a spectacle, perhaps, nobler yet than the spectacle of a united continent, a spectacle which would astonish the world by its novelty and grandeur, the spectacle of two peoples living side by side along a frontier nearly four thousand miles long, with not a cannon, with not a gun frowning across it on either side, with no armaments one against the other, but living in harmony, in mutual confidence and with no other rivalry than a generous emulation in commerce and in the arts of peace." Laurier was right, but he was ahead of his time. In 1911, Canadians were not yet North American enough and not yet sure enough of themselves to lower their guard along the 49th parallel.

When Laurier came back from London, he had decided to ask the people to choose. On July 29, the House was adjourned; the election would take place on September 21, barely three years after the last one. This shows how confident the Liberals were of winning. It was another tactical error. The anti-reciprocity campaign had had its effect, and the Liberals were headed for disaster. Indeed, the campaign would prove particularly painful for them. The government was dragging the weight of fifteen years of being in power and divisive debates, the most recent one being the navy issue. Laurier had lost many of his most stalwart lieutenants, in particular Israël Tarte and Sifton.

The Conservative campaign also received an unexpected boost from south of the border. Comments by some American politicians seemed to confirm the worst fears of the opponents of closer trade ties. For example, the Democratic leader in the House of Representatives, Champ Clark, said, "I am for the bill because I hope to see the day when the American flag will float on every square foot of the British North American possessions clear to the North Pole." President Taft said that Canada "is at a parting of ways," words the opponents of reciprocity were happy to distort.

Borden's Conservatives won the election with a solid majority; in Ontario, they carried seventy-one of the eighty-six ridings. Anti-American prejudice had won out over the letter of the trade agreement. Anti-Catholic and anti-French prejudice had also played a role; there had been a covert campaign against this "papist" prime minister throughout the seven weeks preceding the election. Laurier had made a last-ditch stand. "I am branded in Quebec as a traitor to the French, and in Ontario as a traitor to the English," he said in a speech in Saint John, New Brunswick. "In Quebec I am attacked as an Imperialist, and in Ontario as an anti-Imperialist. I am neither. I am a Canadian. Canada has been the inspiration of my life. I have had before me as a pillar of fire by night and a pillar of cloud by day a policy of true Canadianism, of moderation, of conciliation." To no avail. After fifteen years in power, Wilfrid Laurier had to step down. "We have lost our friends, power, popularity, but I regret nothing," he said. "We have sown the seed: we shall see it germinate." Rather than saving his government from going under, the reciprocity agreement he had negotiated with the United States had pushed it onto the reefs.

The agreement did not bring President Taft any luck either. He was not able to get the reciprocity law adopted until after the election of a Democratic majority in Congress. The Republican Party split, with former president Theodore Roosevelt opposing the nomination of his friend and successor. Right in the middle of this violent internal dispute, Taft published letters he and Roosevelt had exchanged a few days before the announcement of the reciprocity agreement. Taft stated in his letter that the agreement would have the effect of making Canada "only an adjunct of the United States. It would transfer all their important business to Chicago and New York, with their bank credits and everything else, and it would increase greatly the demand of Canada for our manufactures." This again appeared to confirm the Canadians' fears. It is not clear whether Taft really believed that reciprocity would eventually lead to economic, if not political, annexation of Canada. In public, he had always argued that "the talk of annexation is bosh. The United States has all it can attend to with the territory it now has." At any rate, the publication of that correspondence came as a bombshell in Canada and Great Britain. In London, the *Daily Mail* denounced what it saw as a plot against Canada. Laurier was visibly embarrassed. It would be a long time before the seed he thought he had sown in favour of reciprocity would germinate.

Surprisingly, two weeks after his defeat, Laurier did not attribute it to the reciprocity agreement: "It is the province of Ontario which has defeated us. Other losses elsewhere were not very serious and would simply have reduced our majority, but Ontario went solid against us. It is becoming more and more manifest to me that it was not reciprocity that was turned down, but a Catholic premier. All the information which comes to me from that province makes this quite evident." The sophisticated electoral polls political scientists use today did not exist a century ago, so it is impossible to say whether Laurier's interpretation was correct. But it does not seem very likely. Certainly, there was prejudice against him, and his adversaries did not hesitate to exploit it. However, he had confronted and defeated that prejudice in the past. There was no doubt that the defeat was above all due to Ontario; twenty-four of the forty-eight seats lost by the Liberals were in that province. But to blame this result solely on religious intolerance was too easy; it was a way for Laurier to ignore the record of his fifteen years as head of government, a record that was inevitably imperfect. Moreover, the Liberal Party had also lost seventeen seats in the province of Quebec to the unnatural alliance between Borden's Conservatives and Bourassa's nationalists. In that province, the campaign had not been about reciprocity, but about the creation of the Canadian navy. In Ontario, the Conservatives had raised the spectre of annexation, while in Quebec, the nationalists had raised that of conscription.

With this defeat after twenty-four years leading the Liberal Party of Canada, Laurier could finally realize his old dream and return to his Arthabaska residence and his books. He offered the Liberal caucus his resignation, but the MPs' answer was unanimous: they wanted him to stay. Knowing him as we do now, we do not find it surprising that without too much pleading on their part, he agreed to stay on. And he embraced his role as leader of the Opposition with a passion.

THE FINAL CRISIS

Three years later, the First World War broke out. The conscription crisis that occurred during the war was the most painful episode of Laurier's political career. The tensions that re-emerged during that period threatened the two causes to which he had devoted his entire career, almost his entire life: the unity of the country and the unity of the Liberal Party. What a sad ending for the great man, who was now seventy-five years old! But he would play the last act with style, fighting with all the energy he had left, with all his soul, faithful to his principles, pragmatic as always.

From the beginning of the war, Prime Minister Borden had promised on many occasions not to impose conscription. The Imperial Conference that took place in London in the spring of 1917 persuaded him to change his policy. The situation at the front was dire. The conflict, which everyone had expected to be brief, was dragging on. The Canadian forces were being decimated, and recruitment of volunteers was no longer sufficient to make up the losses. At home, there was considerable pressure in favour of conscription. Even within Liberal ranks, many felt that the government should stop at nothing to help the Empire defeat the Germans.

There were also many people who were critical of the fact that Quebec was not contributing its share of troops.

According to data given to the British government at the time, 37.5 percent of Canadian men born in Great Britain had volunteered. The proportion of English-speaking volunteers born in Canada was much lower: 6.5 percent. That of French Canadian men, 1.4 percent, was the lowest of all the white populations in the Empire. In total, there were in the ranks of the Canadian volunteers 162,000 men born in Great Britain, 132,000 English-speaking Canadians, and barely 14,000 French-speaking Canadians.

There were many reasons for the French Canadians' indifference: hostility to any participation in imperial wars, fed for many years by Bourassa's brilliant speeches; the anger of Quebec francophones toward anglophones following the adoption of Regulation 17 banning French from Ontario schools ("Why should we fight for England when the English Canadians want to eliminate French?" asked the nationalists); and a mixture of pacifism and isolationism. Most English Canadians had no sympathy for these reasons or did not understand them. They also refused to acknowledge that the recruitment campaign aimed at francophones had been particularly ham-fisted: the minister of militia and defence, Sam Hughes, was a notorious anti-Catholic, and in some regions of the province of Quebec, recruitment had been entrusted to unilingual anglophone officers. Moreover, there was practically no place for the French language in the armed forces, with a single exception: the creation in 1914 (against Hughes's wishes) of the Royal 22nd Regiment, which was entirely French speaking.

Historians agree that some of the pro-conscription feeling can be attributed to a deplorable hostility toward the francophones of Quebec. In that period, the most vile anti–French Canadian prejudices were expressed openly, with one English-language Montreal newspaper going so far as to call francophones "cockroaches of the kitchen of Canada." In addition to these prejudices, there was a profound and genuine conviction that it was the duty of every British subject to come to the defence of civilization; it was thus felt to be intolerable that French Canadians not do what should be dictated by their conscience.

Prime Minister Borden himself obviously did not understand the francophones' attitude, as this passage from a letter to Sir Charles Tupper shows: "The vision of the French Canadian is very limited. He is not well informed and he is in a condition of extreme exasperation by reason of fancied wrongs supposed to be inflicted upon his compatriots in other provinces, especially Ontario." Was the average English Canadian really better informed than his French-speaking fellow citizens? How could anyone describe the campaigns to eradicate French and the Catholic religion in the West and Ontario as "fancied wrongs"?

One can easily imagine Laurier's sadness at this spectacle. "The racial chasm which is opening at our feet may perhaps not be overcome for many generations," he wrote to Sir George Gibbons, a prominent Liberal. He tried desperately to defend his point of view: if he agreed to conscription when he had sworn to the people of his province since the debate on the navy that there was no question of it, he would be handing Quebec over to Bourassa. The country would never survive that. To the Ontario Liberal leader, N.W. Rowell, he wrote: "Now if I were to waver, to hesitate or to flinch, I would simply hand over the province to the extremists. I would lose the respect of the people whom I thus addressed, and would deserve it. I would not only lose their respect, but my own self-respect also."

Laurier was also against conscription because it conflicted with his Liberal convictions: "All my life I have fought coercion; all my life I have promoted union; and the inspiration that led me to that course shall be my guide at all times so long as there is a breath left in my body," he said in the Commons before the Military Service Bill was adopted. Resorting to a familiar tactic, he appealed to British tradition: "If ever there was a principle which was embedded in the very soil of Britain, it was that the King could demand no service of his people except for the protection of their land and the repelling of invasion. The English people were always afraid of permanent armies."

His suggestion for breaking the deadlock seems extraordinarily naïve: a referendum. Ironically, that was what Bourassa's nationalists had called for during the Boer War and the debate on the navy, and Laurier had rejected the idea. Now he was the one putting it forward. He explained to Rowell: "Let the people decide, and if they decide in favour of conscription, as it seems to me they will …, whatever influence I may have will be employed in pleading to the Quebec people that the question is settled by the verdict of the majority, and that all must loyally accept the issue and submit to the law. And this will be no light task, but a task to which I will devote myself with all my energy." In the House of Commons, he expressed the opinion that a referendum would produce "union and universal satisfaction all round." How could a man of so much experience believe such nonsense? What was the point of consulting the people when the result was already obvious: Quebec would vote overwhelmingly against conscription while in the rest of the country the majority would support it. The crisis would only be exacerbated.

In fact, Laurier knew that full well. Why, then, did he choose the referendum route? Probably because it was the only option that would allow him to gain time. Playing for time was his favourite tactic, and one that had served him well throughout his career. Except that in 1917, not being in power, he was not in control of the tactic, and he was not in control of the timing.

As always, Laurier tried to rise above racial prejudices when examining the problem. He pointed out to those who deplored the indifference of francophone Quebecers that other groups of Canadians also enlisted in small numbers. This was the case, for example, with farmers throughout the country, who realized that conscription would deprive farms of their best manpower. Why, then, attack only francophones? he asked. His arguments went unheeded. Even within his own party, there was pressure to support conscription. He held his ground.

Laurier was convinced that the war was just and that all Canadians who were able to volunteer should do so. He never missed an occasion to encourage his fellow French Canadians to enlist. He tried to move them by invoking the fate of the mother country, France. "There are people who say we will not fight for England; will you then fight for France?" he challenged them at a rally in Montreal. "If I were young like you and had the same health that I enjoy today, I would join those brave Canadians fighting today for the liberation of French territory. I would not have it said that the French-Canadians do less for the liberation of France than the citizens of British origin." He convinced no one.

Laurier became even more isolated when Prime Minister Borden proposed to form a government of national unity. He pretended to consider it and negotiate. Once again he was playing for time, assessing his support and trying to discourage Liberals attracted to the idea of a coalition. Finally, he rejected Borden's proposal. Nine Liberals, including three members of Parliament, decided to join the Tories. On October 12, 1917, Robert Borden announced the formation of the Union Government. Two weeks later, he called a general election.

The election campaign was extremely rough. There was a single issue: conscription. The Unionists did not hesitate to accuse anyone opposed to it of abandoning the Canadian troops at the front, abandoning England, abandoning civilization. The attacks against Laurier and French Canadians were vicious. There were posters that read "A vote for Laurier is a vote for the Kaiser." Quebec, declared one Unionist politician, is "the plague-spot of the whole Dominion." The *Daily News* of Toronto published a map of Canada in which Quebec was coloured black and described as a "foul blot on Canada." According to historians J.L. Granatstein and J.M. Hitsman, this campaign is the only one in Canadian history that was "deliberately conducted on racist grounds." Elizabeth Armstrong, another historian, says, "Surely racial hysteria has seldom reached a higher pitch."

In spite of his prestige, in spite of the affection many Canadians still had for him, Laurier could not withstand the campaign. The winds of imperialist emotion swept away everything in their path. The results on December 17 were catastrophic for what remained of the Liberal Party. The Unionist government won 153 seats and the Liberals only 82, of which 62 were in Quebec. It was the worst outcome imaginable for Laurier, after having sought throughout his career to unite Canadians beyond language and race, to find his support limited to his own province. Moreover, the Liberals had received the backing of Henri Bourassa, who had said: "We ask for nothing better than to help Mr. Laurier overturn the government of national betrayal." That his only remaining ally should be the leader of the nationalists was the unkindest cut of all.

Here, then, was Wilfrid Laurier, in the twilight of his life, with the great dream of his life in tatters. However, while the conscription crisis denied him a chance to return to power and left his party and his country battered and bruised, subsequent events would prove him right. The Military Service Bill had done much more harm to Canada than it had done good for the allied war effort. After months of recruiting, applications for exemptions, hearings in special courts, and searches for deserters; after deadly riots in Montreal and Quebec City; after millions of dollars spent, Canada was able to send only twenty-four thousand additional soldiers to the front—one-quarter of the number Borden had hoped for. Of the conscripts, 23 percent were French Canadians, far less than their proportion of the country's population. "You will find when the war is over that it will be difficult to undo the mischief which has been done," wrote Laurier to a pro-Liberal soldier at the beginning of 1918. "It would have been far easier to have the men by voluntary enlistment, if the government had applied itself to the task with some judgment."

After the gruelling election campaign of 1917, Laurier may have had a moment of discouragement, but if so, it did not last long. And he gave no indication of it publicly or in his correspondence: "I still have faith in the sound sense of the Canadian people and in the broad forces that make for national unity on a base of fair and respecting partnership. Once the war is over, no election, no dozen elections, no unscrupulous propaganda, can prevent Canadians more and more becoming Canadians first, and when they are so, we shall hear less and less of Ontario and of Québec."

One question remains: if Laurier had been in power in 1917, what would he have done? Would he have resisted the tide in favour of conscription at the risk of losing power? Would he have defended the French Canadians and farmers who were opposed to conscription, regardless of the political cost? Much more probably, he would have tried to forge some kind of compromise. Clearly, a referendum would not have settled anything. A quarter-century later, his successor, William Lyon Mackenzie King, would learn that lesson, to his regret.

CHAPTER 7

The Blank

When my eyes close, I hope it will be on a united Canada,
cherishing an abundant hope for the future.
WILFRID LAURIER, 1904

On November 11, 1918, Germany surrendered and the First
World War ended. From that moment on, the days of the
Union Government were numbered; the Liberals who had
joined Borden were thinking about returning to the Liberal
fold. And at the age of seventy-seven, Wilfrid Laurier went
to work with surprising energy to rebuild his party.

At a political meeting in Ottawa at the beginning of
1919, a few days before Parliament was to resume sitting,
the elderly leader began to bind the wounds: "There is not
a man in the party who will say that I tried to influence his
conscience. If his judgment is against me, he is still my
friend. If we have differed in the recent past—upon merely
a transient question which will not arise again—I say let
the past be forgotten. Let us all be Liberals again, actuated
only by conscience. If a man comes to me and says 'I was

a Unionist at the last election,' I will tell him 'I won't rebuke you. You have rebuked yourself enough already.' I will put his hand in mine and look at the future as the only horizon for us." This openness toward those who had abandoned him during the conscription battle was not only strategic; as we know, it was in the man's nature. The same is true of his ambiguity, as shown in this passage on the succession of the leadership of the party, a subject no one dared bring up openly, but that was in all their minds: "Gladly would I have yielded the position to a younger leader and I would do readily today, but so long as God gives me health—it is not as good as it might be, but there is a kick left in me which I can use on occasions—I will stay in the ranks and do my share, lieutenant or private. No matter what is my duty I will do it cheerfully and happily, and nothing would give me greater satisfaction than to stand as a private under a younger general." Was he considering resigning or not? No one could say.

Twelve days later, Henri Bourassa's wife died after a long illness. Laurier made sure to write a sympathy note to the man he had fought so fiercely. The gesture touched the nationalist leader.

On Saturday, February 14, 1919, Laurier had lunch at the Canadian Club and then went to his office in the

Victoria Museum, which had been used for Parliament since a fire destroyed the main building on Parliament Hill in 1916. In the late afternoon, while going through his voluminous correspondence, he felt ill. He stood up, and immediately collapsed. When he got to his feet again, he realized his forehead had been slightly injured. He probably did not suspect that he had had a stroke. Instead of having his car pick him up early, he went home by streetcar.

The next morning when he was getting ready to go to Mass, Laurier had a second episode. Dr. Rodolphe Chevrier, a surgeon at the Ottawa General Hospital, rushed to him. The diagnosis was a cerebral hemorrhage with paralysis. There was talk of administering the last rites to him. Laurier opened his eyes and said, "That is all right, but I'm not as sick as you think, I only feel weak." The priest came. He made the sign of the cross on Laurier's forehead with holy oil and recited the last rites in a low voice: "Per istam sanctam ..." Later, in another brief moment of consciousness, Wilfrid squeezed the hand of his dear good Zoé and murmured, "This is the end."*

* Laurier's biographers do not agree on this point. According to his friend Laurent-Olivier David, his last words, except for whatever occurred between him and the priest who administered the last rites, were, "I only feel weak." Others say that the dying man whispered to Zoé, "It's over" or "This is the end," but the original source of this information is unknown.

Around midnight, he suffered a third stroke. Dr. Chevrier issued a news release stating that Sir Wilfrid had had another cerebral hemorrhage and that the situation appeared hopeless. The doctor was not mistaken. Sir Wilfrid Laurier passed away on Monday, February 17, 1919, shortly before 3 P.M.

THE SADNESS OF A PEOPLE

"When the hour of final rest comes," he had said in 1887, "when my eyes close forever, if I may pay myself this tribute, this simple tribute of having contributed to healing a single patriotic wound in the heart of a single one of my compatriots, of having thus advanced, as little as may be, the cause of unity, concord and harmony among the citizens of this country, then I will believe that my life has not been entirely in vain." Laurier could rest in peace.

The body lay in state in Victoria Museum, from which the desks of all the members of Parliament had been removed, except that of the deceased, on which a wreath of flowers had been placed. Public feeling was strong, surprising even Laurier's most fervent supporters. Photographs show tens of thousands of Canadians filing past his coffin. On February 22, a hundred thousand people lined the streets and gathered at Notre Dame Cemetery in Ottawa for the state funeral. From Paris, where he was taking part in the negotiation of the Treaty of Versailles, Prime Minister Robert Borden wrote: "All Canada will mourn his loss and those who differed from him will be profoundly conscious that his death leaves in the public life of our country a blank that cannot be entirely filled." Even foreign commentators were caught up in the emotion. *The New York Times* wrote: "He seemed to belong to the generation of Disraeli, of Palmerston and of Gladstone."

During the Mass in the Ottawa basilica, the first archbishop of Regina, Msgr. Olivier-Elzéar Mathieu, marvellously summed up the political philosophy of the illustrious departed: "No one understood better than he that there are hundreds of questions on which honest people have the right to be divided and the duty to forgive each other for those divisions; that political issues are so complicated, especially in a country such as ours, that their solution, in practice, depends on so many diverse circumstances that it frequently occurs that men moved by the same desire to serve their homeland can be in disagreement as to the means to use to reach that goal; that the diverse nationalities that compete for influence and predominance over our huge territory are not obliged to be each other's enemies, because competition does not imply rivalry, much less antipathy, and concord does not imply fusion. Why, then, should we not unite without assimilating? Why should we not live in harmony, preserving in all its purity, even improving, the blood of the two beautiful nations that have written the most glorious pages of our history? Why not live in harmony, remembering that most nations have been formed out of heterogeneous elements, just as their flags are made of strips of silk or wool sewn together?"

Among those attending the ceremony was Laurier's old adversary Henri Bourassa, who praised him as follows in *Le Devoir:* "The private virtues of the eminent statesman, his admirable qualities of the heart, that tireless, modest charity, the great dignity of his life, are reasons for trust and consolation for all those who loved him. And who among those who knew him, supporter or adversary, did not love him, could fail to love him?" Who, indeed?

THE LEGACY

What is our situation now, almost a century after Wilfrid Laurier's death? In these decades, Canada has experienced dramatic economic and demographic growth, becoming one of the most envied countries in the world. Our history has been marked by significant tensions, particularly between anglophones and francophones, but these tensions have been dealt with peacefully, by democratic means. This is an exceptional achievement, especially during times when millions of people in the world have fallen victim to ethnic, religious, and political violence.

The risk of Quebec's separation seems to have been averted in the short term. However, another phenomenon has been developing, which poses an equal threat to the future of Canada: mutual indifference. The fact that most of the Quebec members of the House of Commons are from the Bloc Québécois means that the role of Quebec francophones in federal institutions is diminished. In the long run, this is harmful for Quebec and for the whole country. Quebecers see themselves less and less in a federal government in which they are no longer as well represented as they once were: it is, as the proponents of independence repeat with some truth, "the government of another nation." Quebecers do not want to leave Canada, but neither are they interested in participating in its governance.

One also senses in English Canada a great weariness with regard to Quebec, a mixture of indifference, impatience, and hostility. This attitude may be understandable in view of the tensions that have marked our history. Nevertheless, it represents a significant danger for the future of this country, which was founded on the idea of an alliance between two language groups. The couple is not divorcing, but it is not getting along well and is sleeping in separate bedrooms.

If he were with us today, Sir Wilfrid would be disheartened to see how little progress we have made in creating the shared nationality that he aspired to. The first French Canadian to become prime minister of the country, he showed francophones that they could play a leading role, not only in the province of Quebec but from sea to sea. The successor of LaFontaine and Cartier, he blazed a trail for St-Laurent, Trudeau, Mulroney, and Chrétien. Who would have thought that, after seeing several of their own excel as leaders of Canada, francophone Quebecers would lose interest in the country they had founded and contributed so much to shaping?

Laurier proved to English Canadians who doubted it that francophones were just as capable as anyone of governing Canada. Certainly, Laurier was a victim of prejudices. But his four electoral victories and the outpouring of emotion when he died show that, beyond differences of language and religion, millions of people throughout the country had great admiration and affection for this Catholic French Canadian from Saint-Lin, Quebec. And yet, a century later, prejudices against francophone Quebecers have not completely disappeared.

Does the persistence of tensions between francophones and anglophones mean that Laurier failed in his work? Yes and no. Yes, because the Canadian patriotism he wanted to see emerge has not made the progress he hoped in his native province. No, because the reality never lives up to the ideal—but that is no reason to give up on the ideal. You may, for a moment, dream of withdrawing to your peaceful Arthabaska. But once this moment of discouragement is past, you have to roll up your sleeves again and get back to work. A federation will always be a project, a work in progress. Contrary to the standard often imposed on federal systems, their success cannot be measured by the absence of conflict. Because in essence a federation unites people of different cultures and/or regions, disagreements are inevitable. A federal system works well if it can manage these tensions peacefully and productively. By this yardstick, the Canadian federation is a model.

For work on the project to continue, for the country to stand firm against the McCarthys and Bourassas who will always beset it, we need leaders who are clear-sighted, moderate, and charismatic. Laurier set an example, tracing the only path that could ensure the future of Confederation, the path of compromise and respect for diversity. What he said then is equally valid today: to resolve our conflicts, we have to rely on the "sunny ways" of negotiation and the higher principles of democracy, justice, and federalism. Federalism today is too often seen as a system of tedious and sometimes dysfunctional institutions, but we should never lose sight of the attitude and culture of openness and dialogue that are at its core. At a time when continents and countries have to deal with unprecedented diversity, federalism is the most modern and attractive system there is. A fundamentally tolerant and moderate man, Laurier was, better than anyone else, able to live up to the standard of this authentic federalism.

For the Canadian union to endure, we also need to cultivate Canadian patriotism—a patriotism that transcends rather than smothers regional feelings—thus adding the warmth of emotion to the cold, dispassionate principles. A romantic orator, Laurier was able to blow on those embers. Canadian patriotism is based in part on the relationship of the country with the rest of the world. The stature Sir Wilfrid achieved on the international stage brought English Canada and French Canada together in a shared feeling of pride. This was the birth of a national feeling in Canada, a very significant step. Our politicians today would do well to remember the lesson that the best way to forge links among Canadians is by adopting a foreign policy that is in keeping with their shared values and hopes.

From the point of view of French Canada, which one was right, Laurier or Bourassa? The federation has survived many crises since their battles. However, the assimilation of francophones outside Quebec has continued, and the dream of a country where the two main cultural groups would live in perfect harmony from sea to sea, a dream shared by these two men, is still only a dream. Nevertheless, Laurier saw clearly that a country founded on compromise can survive only by continuing in that spirit. Moreover, was Bourassa wrong to focus on the rights of minorities and equality between the two main founding peoples?

In fact, the two men complemented one another. One might say Bourassa was Laurier's conscience; without him, Laurier would perhaps have made too many concessions and thus, unintentionally, allowed those who wanted to eradicate the French fact in Canada to triumph. "Since it is the minority that is asked to make most of the sacrifices and concessions," wrote Laurent-Olivier David, "the public men who represent it constantly ask how far they can go on the path of conciliation without offending their conscience or public sentiment, without violating a right or a principle." Bourassa was always watchful of Laurier to make sure he did not go so far on that path that he would lose sight of the interests of his "race." No doubt this is always the case: those who govern must seek practical solutions, but we also need people who fight for honour, for the "heroic solution." Out of the tension between the two, a tension that sometimes seems unbearable, comes a middle course. The history of French Canada is marked by these duels: LaFontaine and Papineau, Cartier and Dorion, Laurier and Bourassa, Lapointe and Duplessis, Trudeau and Lévesque, Mulroney and Bouchard. What political scientist Gérard Bergeron said of Trudeau and Lévesque is true of all these dialectical pairs: "Each one, in its own way, illustrates the difficulty of preserving a French culture in this America that is so massively anglophone. In this they are Us, magnificently and terribly."

Is there not in the belated but sincere reconciliation of Laurier and Bourassa a lesson for all those who defend their ideas on the future of Canada and Quebec? Wouldn't it be preferable, wouldn't it be more Canadian, to debate without using extreme language, making personal attacks, or imputing motives? "The next time you are in town, dear friend, come and see me and we'll talk about it," Laurier often wrote to his adversaries. Canada would be better off today if we were more willing to listen to each other.

Our country is lucky to have been governed by some great leaders in the course of the last century. However, I do not think any of them reflected as well as Laurier did the attitudes of moderation and openness to dialogue that make this country possible and that, human nature being what it is, are so easily abandoned. Not only was Laurier convinced of the importance of these values, he lived them. He was, in his whole being, fair, open to others, and pragmatic. In addition, he was profoundly convinced of the exceptional destiny of that young country called Canada and of the duty of those living in it to overcome their differences so as not to betray that destiny. Wilfrid Laurier personified the Canadian vision.

That is why a person examining the life of this extraordinary Canadian and observing the sad political scene of our day can only conclude that Borden was right: the blank left by Laurier's passing was never filled.

BIBLIOGRAPHY

Alverstone, Richard Everard Webster, Viscount. *Recollections of Bar and Bench.* London: Edward Arnold, 1915.

Asselin, Olivar. *Emigration from Belgium and France to Canada.* Ottawa: King's Printer (Department of the Interior), 1913.

Barthe, Ulric, ed. *Wilfrid Laurier on the Platform, 1871–1890.* Quebec: Turcotte & Menard, 1890.

Bélanger, Réal. *Wilfrid Laurier: Quand la politique devient passion.* Quebec: Presses de l'Université Laval, 2007.

Bernard, Jean-Paul. *Les Rouges: Libéralisme, nationalisme et anti-cléricalisme au milieu du XIXe siècle.* Montreal: Presses de l'Université du Québec, 1971.

Bliss, Michael. *Right Honourable Men: The Descent of Canadian Politics from Macdonald to Mulroney.* Toronto: HarperCollins, 1994.

Brown, Robert Craig, and Ramsay Cook. *Canada 1896–1921: A Nation Transformed.* Toronto: McClelland and Stewart, 1991.

Careless, J.M.S. *Canada, A Story of Challenge.* Toronto: Macmillan of Canada, 1972.

Crunican, Paul. *Priests and Politicians: Manitoba Schools and the Election of 1896.* Toronto: University of Toronto Press, 1974.

Dafoe, J.W. *Laurier: A Study in Canadian Politics.* Echo Library, 2007.

Dandurand, Raoul. *Raoul Dandurand, le sénateur-diplomate: Mémoires 1861–1942.* Quebec: Presses de l'Université Laval, 2000.

David, Laurent-Olivier. *Laurier et son temps.* Montreal: La Patrie éditeurs, 1905.

———. *Laurier: sa vie, ses oeuvres.* Beauceville: L'Éclaireur éditeurs, 1919.

DeCelles, Alfred D. *Discours de Sir Wilfrid Laurier.* 2 vol. Montreal: Librairie Beauchemin, 1920.

Ellis, Lewis E. *Reciprocity 1911: A Study in Canadian-American Relations.* New Haven: Yale University Press, 1939.

Fisher, Charles. *Dearest Émilie: The Love-Letters of Sir Wilfrid Laurier to Madame Émilie Lavergne.* Toronto: NC Press, 1989.

Granatstein, J.L., and J.M. Hitsman. *Broken Promises: A History of Conscription in Canada.* Toronto: Oxford University Press, 1977.

Hall, David J. *Clifford Sifton.* 2 vol. Vancouver: University of British Columbia Press, 1981/1985.

Hart, Michael. *A Trading Nation: Canadian Trade Policy from Colonialism to Globalization.* Vancouver: University of British Columbia Press, 2002.

Hilliker, John, and Donald Barry. *Canada's Department of External Affairs: The Early Years, 1909–1946.* Montreal: McGill-Queen's University Press, 1990.

Hommage à Henri Bourassa. Reprinted from a commemorative issue of *Le Devoir,* October 25, 1952.

LaPierre, Laurier L. *Sir Wilfrid Laurier and the Romance of Canada.* Toronto: Stoddart, 1996.

Lower, Arthur R.M. *Colony to Nation: A History of Canada.* Toronto: Longmans, Green & Company, 1947.

Munro, John A. *The Alaska Boundary Dispute.* Toronto: Copp Clark, 1970.

Neatby, H. Blair. *Laurier and a Liberal Quebec: A Study in Political Management.* Toronto: McClelland and Stewart, 1973.

Neatby, H. Blair, et al., ed. *Imperial Relations in the Age of Laurier: Essays.* Toronto: University of Toronto Press, 1969.

Pacaud, Lucien, ed. *Sir Wilfrid Laurier: Letters to My Father and Mother.* Toronto: Ryerson, 1935.

Penlington, Norman. *The Alaska Boundary Dispute: A Critical Reappraisal.* Toronto: McGraw-Hill Ryerson, 1972.

Rumilly, Robert. *Henri Bourassa: La vie publique d'un grand Canadien.* Montreal: Éditions Chantecler, 1953.

———. *Laurier.* Vol. VIII of *Histoire de la province de Québec.* Montreal: Éditions Bernard Valiquette, 1942.

Schull, Joseph. *Laurier: The First Canadian.* Toronto: Macmillan of Canada, 1965.

Silver, Arthur I. *The French-Canadian Idea of Confederation 1864–1900.* Toronto: University of Toronto Press, 1997.

Skelton, Oscar Douglas. *Life and Letters of Sir Wilfrid Laurier.* 2 vol. London: Humphrey Milford, Oxford University Press, 1922.

Stevens, George Roy. *History of the Canadian National Railways.* Toronto: Collier-Macmillan Canada, 1973.

Voisine, Nive, and Jean Hamelin, ed. *Les Ultramontains canadiens-français.* Montreal: Boréal Express, 1985.

Willison, John. *Sir Wilfrid Laurier.* London and Toronto: Oxford University Press, 1926.

———. *Reminiscences, Political and Personal.* Kessinger Publishing Legacy Reprints, 2007.

The author also consulted Wilfrid Laurier's correspondence at Library and Archives Canada, as well as the House of Commons debates (Hansard).

ACKNOWLEDGMENTS

This book would not have been possible without the generous and diligent assistance of my elder son, Vincent Laurin-Pratte, who spent hours reading Laurier's correspondence in order to find letters that might be useful to me. My other son, François, was also of invaluable help to me with encouragement, advice, and support in everyday life.

My assistant at *La Presse* for the past ten years, Christiane Clermont, was also a great help. Christiane is the most friendly, generous, and efficient person I have ever had the good fortune to encounter in journalism.

Guy Crevier, CEO and publisher of *La Presse*, was kind enough to allow me to devote time to this peculiar extracurricular activity. Réal Bélanger, Laurier LaPierre, the Honourable Serge Joyal, and Jean-Claude Robert took the time to read my manuscript and gave me the benefit of their extensive knowledge.

It was John Ralston Saul who had the strange idea of entrusting me with the writing of this book. He explained that the task would be an extraordinary learning opportunity. Mr. Saul was right, and I am grateful to him for that, as well as for his advice.

I would like to thank everyone who assisted me with my research, in particular Caroline Jamet, vice-president for communications at *La Presse;* Sophie Grenier, librarian at Library and Archives Canada; Bernard Roche, Cultural Resource Manager, Laurier House National Historic Site, in Ottawa; and Nicole Tremblay, Director of the Bibliothèque des lettres et sciences humaines at the Université de Montréal. I also wish to thank the very helpful personnel of the Bibliothèque nationale du Québec in Montreal, in particular the staff of the Centre d'archives de Montréal.

Finally, all my gratitude and love go to my wife, Anne Marie, who allowed Wilfrid Laurier to live with us, and sometimes between us, for three years. Anne Marie and I have been married for thirty years. I look forward happily to the prospect of our surpassing the fifty years of marriage of Zoé and Wilfrid.

1841   Proclamation of the Act of Union, uniting the
            colonies of Lower Canada and Upper Canada
            in a single Province of Canada.

            Birth of Wilfrid Laurier in the village of Saint-
            Lin, Quebec.

1847–1852   Laurier attends elementary school in Saint-Lin.

1852–1854   Laurier attends English school in New
            Glasgow, Quebec.

1854–1861   Laurier studies at Collège de L'Assomption.

1861–1864   Laurier studies law at McGill University,
            Montreal.

1864   Laurier becomes a lawyer.

1866   Because of his fragile health, Laurier leaves
            Montreal to become the editor of the news-
            paper *Le Défricheur* in the village of L'Avenir in
            the Eastern Townships. He later moves to
            Victoriaville, and then to Arthabaskaville,
            where he opens a law office.

1867   The British North America Act comes into
            force, creating the Canadian Confederation.

1868   Laurier marries Zoé Lafontaine.

1871   Laurier is elected to the Quebec Legislative
            Assembly, representing Drummond-
            Arthabaska.

1874   In the wake of the Pacific Scandal, which
            forced the resignation of Conservative prime
            minister John A. Macdonald, the Liberal Party
            led by Alexander Mackenzie wins the general
            election. As a Liberal candidate in Drummond-
            Arthabaska, Laurier is elected to the House of
            Commons.

1877   Laurier is appointed minister of inland revenue
            in the government of Alexander Mackenzie.

            In Quebec City, he gives his now famous
            speech on liberalism.

            Defeated in a by-election in Drummond-
            Arthabaska, he is later elected MP for Quebec
            East.

1878   The Mackenzie government is defeated;
            the Conservatives return to power led by

	John A. Macdonald. Laurier is re-elected in Quebec East.
1882	General election. Macdonald is returned to power. Laurier is again re-elected.
1885	Accused of treason following the North-West Rebellion, the Métis leader Louis Riel is hanged.
1887	General election. The Conservatives win again. Laurier remains MP for Quebec East.
	Edward Blake resigns as leader of the Liberal Party; Laurier succeeds him.
1890	The Manitoba legislature abolishes confessional schools in favour of a single network of public schools and makes English the only official language in the province.
1891	General election. Another victory for Macdonald's Conservatives.
	Death of John A. Macdonald.
1896	General election. The Liberals win, bringing to an end eighteen years of Conservative government. Wilfrid Laurier becomes the first French Canadian to serve as prime minister of Canada.

Laurier–Greenway agreement on the Manitoba schools.

1897   Laurier makes his mark at the first Imperial Conference, in London.

1899–1902   The Boer War. To assist the British, the Laurier government equips and transports two divisions of volunteer troops. Henri Bourassa leaves the Liberal caucus in protest.

1900   General election. The Liberals are returned to power with an increased majority.

1903   The arbitration tribunal on the boundaries of Alaska decides in favour of the United States. The decision causes an outcry in Canada.

Laurier presents to the House his plan for a second transcontinental railway.

1904   General election. The Liberal Party again increases its majority.

1905   Creation of the provinces of Saskatchewan and Alberta through the Autonomy Bills. Laurier tries to protect the right of Catholics to separate schools, but is forced to back down.

1908   General election. The Liberals win.

1910   Adoption of the Naval Service Act.

1911   Conclusion of a trade reciprocity agreement
            between Canada and the United States.

            General election. Robert Borden's
            Conservatives win, in part thanks to a deal
            struck with Bourassa's Quebec nationalists.
            Laurier returns to the House as Leader of the
            official Opposition.

1912   The government of Ontario adopts
            Regulation 17, limiting the teaching of French
            in the province.

1914–1918   World War One.

1917   Borden tables the Military Service Bill to
            introduce conscription.

            Formation of a Union Government, which
            includes nine Liberals.

            General election. Borden's Unionists defeat
            Laurier's Liberals. The Liberal Party is deci-
            mated everywhere except in Quebec.

1919   Sir Wilfrid Laurier dies in his Ottawa
            residence.